NO GALLBLADDER GUIDE AND COOKBOOK

Transform Your Diet and Balance Your Metabolism after Gallbladder Removal with Simple and Delicious Recipes, Effective Guidelines and a 28-Day Meal Plan.

Emma Greenfield

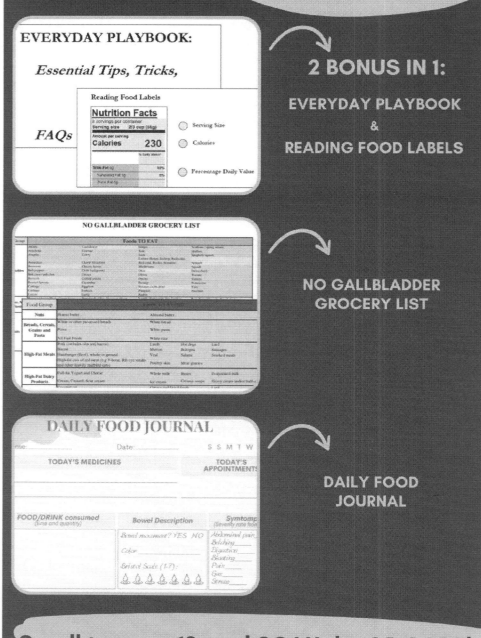

3 + 1 EXTRA BONUS

INSIDE THE BOOK

EVERYDAY PLAYBOOK:

Essential Tips, Tricks,

FAQs

2 BONUS IN 1:

EVERYDAY PLAYBOOK
&
READING FOOD LABELS

NO GALLBLADDER
GROCERY LIST

DAILY FOOD
JOURNAL

Scroll to page 19, and SCAN the QR CODE!

Table of Content

4.10 Smoothies and Beverages Recipes

CHAPTER 5: SPECIAL OCCASION RECIPES

CHAPTER 6: A 28-DAY MEAL PLAN FOR A GALLBLADDER-FREE LIFESTYLE

Introduction

Purpose and Motivation Behind the Book

Welcome to the No Gallbladder Guide and Cookbook, where culinary delight meets mindful nutrition for those who've undergone gallbladder removal and the loved ones who support them.

The gallbladder, a small organ sitting below the liver, might seem insignificant, but its removal can have a profound impact on daily life, especially when it comes to nutrition. As someone who's had the surgery, or as a caring friend or family member, you might feel overwhelmed by dietary restrictions, lingering symptoms, and a myriad of unanswered questions. This book seeks to be your companion, offering guidance, understanding, and of course, delicious recipes tailored for a post-gallbladder lifestyle.

Central to this book is the joy of food. Beyond being a practical guide, this is a celebration of gastronomy tailored for a post-gallbladder lifestyle. We've curated recipes that aren't just nutritious but are also a feast for the senses. Imagine dishes that burst with color, aroma, and flavor, all while being gentle on your digestive system. And the best part? These culinary delights come without the usual fuss. Our recipes are designed to be easy-to-prepare, ensuring that even those new to the kitchen feel like seasoned chefs.

But we also recognize the importance of understanding. While the heart of this book beats to the rhythm of delightful recipes, its soul lies in the knowledge it offers. We delve into the science of post-gallbladder nutrition, ensuring that with every dish you prepare, you do so with confidence and understanding.

While this book leans heavily into the joy of cooking, it also serves as a beacon for those navigating the nuances of life post-surgery. Each page is a testament to the belief that dietary changes need not be daunting but can instead be a delightful voyage of discovery.

So, let's embark on this gastronomic adventure together, discovering new flavors, understanding our bodies better, and savoring every bite with confidence and joy. Welcome to a new world of delightful dining!

Chapter 1: Understanding the Gallbladder

1.1 Overview of Gallbladder Function

Nestled beneath the liver, the gallbladder is a small, pear-shaped organ. Its primary role is to store bile, a digestive fluid produced by the liver. This fluid aids in the breakdown and absorption of fats in the food we consume.

Whenever we eat foods, especially those rich in fats, the gallbladder releases the stored bile into the small intestine. Here, bile emulsifies the fats, breaking them down into smaller droplets, making them more accessible to digestive enzymes. Think of it as nature's dish detergent, helping to break down and remove oily substances. In essence, without the gallbladder's regular release of bile, digesting fatty foods becomes a challenge.

1.2 Common Reasons for Gallbladder Removal

There are several reasons one might need to bid farewell to their gallbladder:

- **Gallstones**: These are hardened deposits that can form in the gallbladder, and interrupt the smooth flow of bile, leading to pain and potential complications.
- **Cholecystitis**: This condition refers to the inflammation of the gallbladder, primarily resulting from obstructions like gallstones.
- **Polyps**: These are non-cancerous growths within the organ. Although usually harmless, larger polyps can cause complications, necessitating removal.
- **Gallbladder cancer**: While uncommon, malignancies within the gallbladder can also lead to its removal as a measure to prevent further complications or spread.

1.3 Overview of Gallbladder Surgery and Recovery

The surgical procedure to remove the gallbladder is known as a cholecystectomy. It's a widely performed surgery with two primary methods: open surgery and laparoscopic (keyhole) surgery. The latter is less invasive, resulting in smaller scars and typically faster recovery times.

Hospital stays vary depending on the surgery type and individual recovery rates, but many patients return home within a day or two post-laparoscopic surgery.

After the surgery, it's common to experience mild discomfort and fatigue. Some patients commonly experience symptoms like indigestion, abdominal pain, and nausea. In addition, bloating or flatulence may also occur. Faecal problems are also common after surgery because of the extra bile in the bowel, and this can make diarrhea worse after eating fatty foods.

1.4 Adapting to a Gallbladder-free Life

Cholecystectomy is a common procedure, and many lead a normal life post-surgery. However, the body must adapt to the absence of the gallbladder.

It's this shift that necessitates dietary adjustments, which we'll explore in depth as we journey through this book.

Without this organ, bile flows directly into the small intestine, albeit in smaller quantities, and can be laxative. This continuous trickle, rather than the gallbladder's concentrated releases, changes the way our bodies handle fats.

Some individuals experience loose stools, also known as diarrhea, after undergoing this surgery. Typically, the diarrhea lasts for a few weeks to a few months.

If this occurs, there is no particular diet that you must adhere to, but the following tips may help reduce diarrhea after surgery:

- **Watch your fat intake**: The quantity of fat in your diet also affects your digestion. Smaller portions are simpler to digest, while larger amounts may not be fully digested and can lead to flatulence, bloating and diarrhoea. Avoid consuming high-fat foods and opt for foods that contain no more than 3 grams of fat per serving (low-fat) or are fat-free. Examine the labels and adhere to the indicated serving size.
- **Avoid eating large meals**: This can make digestion more difficult and cause bloating. Try to eat every few hours, with smaller, more frequent meals and snacks. To meet all your nutritional needs, eat 4-6 small meals a day. A good diet includes lean meats like chicken, fish and low-fat dairy products in moderation, vegetables, fruit and whole grains.
- **Increase your fiber intake**: To promote regular bowel movements. Incorporating soluble fiber, like oats and barley, can be beneficial, but it is important to gradually increase the amount of fiber over a period of several weeks to avoid exacerbating gas and cramps.

It's important to understand that while the gallbladder has its role, humans can adapt well without it. Our bodies are remarkable in their resilience and ability to adjust. The aim isn't to lament its absence, but to embrace the new dietary landscape, ensuring optimal health and enjoyment in every meal.

Chapter 2: Life After Gallbladder Surgery

2.1 Physiological Changes After Surgery

The aftermath of gallbladder removal ushers in a phase of significant physiological adaptation. The body's innate capability to reconfigure its functions is remarkable, and understanding these changes will arm you with the confidence to navigate this new phase of your health journey.

Bile's New Rhythm
The absence of the gallbladder means that bile, while still diligently produced by the liver, adopts a new flow pattern. Instead of being stored and released in response to meals, particularly fatty ones, bile now flows directly and steadily into the small intestine. This results in a continuous, less concentrated trickle that contrasts with the previously robust, periodic bursts.

Digestive Dynamics Altered
With this constant yet diluted bile flow, the digestive process, especially regarding fats, undergoes transformation. The gallbladder's strategic release of bile ensured a well-timed response to larger fat intakes. Now, without its measured doses, the body leans towards handling smaller, more frequent fat consumption for optimal digestion. This might mean that heavy, fatty meals are digested differently and may sometimes lead to discomfort.

Liver's Elevated Role
Without the gallbladder's intermediary storage function, the liver steps up its role. It still produces the same amount of bile, but now it also manages its consistent release into the digestive system. Over time, the liver and the digestive tract typically adjust to this new rhythm, showcasing the body's resilience.

Sensitivity to Certain Foods
Post-surgery, there may be heightened sensitivity to specific foods, especially those rich in fats or spices. It's common to notice distinct reactions to meals that were previously consumed without a second thought. This heightened sensitivity isn't permanent for everyone, but it signifies the body's way of signaling its new dietary preferences. It is advisable to maintain a food diary to identify and avoid triggers.

2.2 Before Gallbladder Removal Surgery

Patients with hepatic colic and/or gallstones who require a cholecystectomy (removal of the gallbladder) should adhere to a lipid-free (fat-free) diet to prevent the gallbladder from contracting, which could displace the stones and cause potential hepatic colic.

2.3 Post-Surgical Diet for the Gallbladder

Following gallbladder surgery, specific dietary modifications are recommended to align with the body's altered digestive processes.

A. Initial Recovery Phase (First week post-surgery):

Drinking plenty of fluids is very important right after surgery. Diarrhea is common after gallbladder surgery and can quickly dehydrate your body, causing a loss of essential fluids, vitamins, and minerals. To give your body enough time to recover, it is recommended that you limit your intake to liquids.

- **Dietary Approach**: Your doctor might suggest a "clear liquid diet" that includes clear broths, gelatin, juices, and herbal teas for avoiding nausea, vomiting, or constipation. You will start following a simple BRAT diet after a few days, consisting of bread, rice, applesauce, toast, or soda crackers. The diet can assist in managing loose or runny stool in a gentle way. However, a BRAT diet may be unnecessary if you already have normal bowel movements.
- **Recommendations**: Choose clear broths and gradually introduce thicker soups. Make sure to drink plenty of water, broths, and drinks with added vitamins or minerals. Sports drinks are a good choice during this time. It's crucial to avoid alcoholic, carbonated and caffeinated beverages (including coffee, energy drinks, tea).

B. Intermediate Recovery Phase (One to three weeks post-surgery):

- **Dietary Approach:** A soft diet that is low in fats aids in the transition towards regular foods. This approach minimizes potential digestive discomfort. Most people eat three large meals a day (breakfast, lunch, and dinner). But after gallbladder surgery, that's not good for you. It is better to have small meals every 2-3 hours. This will give your body the nutrients and energy it needs without overburdening your liver.
- **Recommendations:** Begin with oatmeal, fish, plain rice, boiled potatoes or sweet potatoes, steamed vegetables and fruits. Refrain from spicy foods and those with high fat content.

C. Extended Recovery and Beyond (One month and onwards):

- **Dietary Approach**: A balanced diet with controlled fat intake can be reintroduced. You should start incorporating healthy fats into your diet on a regular basis after a few weeks, when your body (especially your liver) has adjusted to not having a gallbladder. Observing reactions to different foods is imperative.
- **Recommendations:** Consume lean proteins, whole grains, and vegetables. Avoid eating fried foods, fatty meats, and dairy products. Gradually reintroduce foods and monitor for any adverse reactions.

D. Long-term Dietary Strategy:

- **Dietary Approach**: Focus on maintaining a balanced diet with an emphasis on whole foods. Fat intake should be distributed throughout the day to optimize digestion. After having their gallbladders removed, patients can benefit from a long-term diet that is low in fat and high in fiber. It is also expected that this type of diet will have fewer calories, which may help with weight loss and weight maintenance. Cholecystectomy is associated with an increased risk of liver problems. These include non-alcoholic fatty liver disease. However, this risk is known to be lowered by a diet high in whole grains, legumes, fish, vegetables, and fruits.
- **Recommendations:** Include sources of soluble fiber like oats and fruits, which can assist in stool formation. Opt for healthy fat sources like avocados and nuts while minimizing saturated fats. Ensure regular monitoring and adjustments based on individual tolerances.

2.4 Potential Complications and How to Mitigate Them

Adjusting to life without a gallbladder can be a seamless transition for some, but for others, it may come with a set of challenges. While most people find their new normal within a few weeks to months, it's essential to be aware of potential complications and know how to address them.

Bloating and Gas

As the digestive system gets accustomed to its new flow of bile, some may experience bloating or gas.

→ **Mitigation:** Over-the-counter medications can provide temporary relief. Dietary adjustments, such as reducing the intake of gas-producing foods and slowly reintroducing them, can help the body adjust. Probiotic supplements or foods can also be beneficial in restoring gut flora balance.

Diarrhea or Loose Stools

The continuous trickle of bile into the intestines can sometimes result in more frequent or looser stools.

→ **Mitigation:** A diet rich in soluble fiber, such as found in oats, apples, and bananas, can help firm up stools. Limiting caffeine, spicy foods, and very fatty meals can also alleviate symptoms. If the issue persists, consult a doctor, as medications like bile acid binders might be beneficial.

Digestive Discomfort After Fatty Foods

Without the gallbladder's concentrated bile bursts, heavy fatty meals may be harder to digest, leading to discomfort.

→ **Mitigation:** Spread out fat consumption over the day in smaller amounts. Opt for healthy fats like avocados and olive oil, and consider digestive enzymes supplements that aid in breaking down fats.

Indigestion and Heartburn

Some people might experience a heightened sensitivity, leading to indigestion or heartburn after certain meals.

→ **Mitigation:** Smaller, more frequent meals can reduce the load on the digestive system. Avoiding triggers like spicy foods, caffeine, and alcohol, and not lying down immediately after eating can also help. Over-the-counter antacids can offer relief, but persistent symptoms should prompt a doctor's visit.

Weight Changes

The alteration in bile flow and dietary changes can lead to fluctuations in weight. Some might experience weight loss due to dietary restrictions, while others could see a gain if they lean towards more carbohydrate-heavy meals.

→ **Mitigation:** Maintaining a balanced diet and regular exercise can help stabilize weight. Seeking advice from a nutritionist can provide tailored guidance based on individual needs.

Stay Connected with Healthcare Professionals

While many of the post-surgical symptoms are manageable with dietary adjustments, always consult with healthcare professionals when in doubt or if symptoms persist. Regular check-ups and open communication with your doctor will ensure you navigate this post-surgical journey with confidence.

Chapter 3: Nutritional Foundations

3.1 Nutritional Recommendations

After having surgery to remove the gallbladder, the way one thinks about food changes significantly. Following a specific diet after surgery not only helps the digestive system adjust, but also promotes healing and overall health. It is recommended to consume a diet that is low in animal protein and fat, and high in fiber, especially from vegetables. Begin by consuming a small amount of low-fat and gradually increase your intake, monitoring how well your body tolerates it. It is crucial to drink a sufficient amount of water and steer clear of sugary and fast foods.

As an extra bonus, you'll find a detailed Grocery List, which includes: allowed and forbidden foods, foods to be reintroduced gradually after gallbladder removal, and foods to be eaten occasionally during the normal diet.

We will examine the details of this dietary journey, helping you to choose foods that fit with your body's new routine.

1) Lean and Clean Beginnings

In the immediate aftermath of surgery, the digestive system seeks gentleness. A low-fat diet is the gold standard during this phase, providing sustenance without overburdening the system.

- **Proteins to Prefer:** You can digest protein even without a gallbladder. This means that high-protein foods won't cause any problems unless they're also high in fat. Choose lean cuts of meat and remove any extra fat. Opt for lean meats like chicken or turkey. Fish, especially those rich in omega-3 like salmon, can also be a good addition, but ensure they're grilled, baked, or steamed rather than fried. Some plant proteins include tofu, chickpeas, beans, and peas.
- **Vegetables on the Vanguard:** Non-cruciferous vegetables, such as carrots, zucchini, and spinach, are advised. Preferred preparation methods include steaming or boiling.
- **Grains that Gain:** Whole grains such as brown rice, quinoa, and oatmeal provide necessary energy without overwhelming the digestive system.

2) Fats in Moderation

This may be the hardest diet advice to follow, but it's definitely the most critical. Your body will struggle to digest fat after surgery. Although you'll want to add healthy fats to your diet at some point, the best approach is to stick to an unprocessed, low-fat diet for several weeks after gallbladder removal. Opt for foods like plain toast, rice, bananas, soup, and pasta, without any butter. As the days post-surgery progress and your body signals its readiness, the reintroduction of fats should be gradual. Observing how your body responds to these increments is crucial.

- **Introduction of Healthy Fats:** Avocado slices in a salad, a handful of nuts, or a drizzle of olive oil can be good starting points. Other healthy fats include chia seeds, flaxseeds, almonds, sardines, salmon, and anchovies.
- **Reduction of Saturated and Trans Fats:** Items like fried foods, pastries, and certain margarines (hydrogenated vegetable oils) can be particularly challenging for the post-gallbladder system and might best be consumed sparingly.

3) Carbohydrates

Carbohydrates play an integral role in the post-surgical dietary landscape. As a primary energy source for the body, they support recovery and daily functioning. However, it's essential to differentiate between simple and complex carbohydrates.

- **Simple carbohydrates**, like sugars found in candies and certain beverages, can lead to rapid blood sugar spikes, potentially exacerbating digestive discomfort.
- **Complex carbohydrates**, found in foods like whole grains, legumes, and vegetables, provide sustained energy without causing abrupt digestive or blood sugar challenges. Following gallbladder surgery, it is advisable to prioritize the intake of complex carbohydrates to ensure steady energy levels while minimizing potential digestive disturbances. Whole-grain cereals or oatmeal, whole-grain bread or pasta, and brown rice are good sources of complex carbohydrates.

4) Stay Hydrated and Fiber-Fortified

Optimal hydration is crucial for effective digestion and post-surgical recovery. Concurrently, controlled fiber intake aids in maintaining a smooth digestive tract.

- **Water Consumption:** Aim for at least 8 glasses a day. Infuse with slices of cucumber or citrus fruits for added flavor and nutrients.
- **Controlled Fiber Introduction:** While fiber is essential, introducing it too rapidly can cause gas or discomfort. Opt for soluble fiber sources initially, like apples, pears, prunes, and oats. Gradually integrate more high fiber sources as your body adjusts, such as wheat bran, legumes and berries.

5) The Dairy Dilemma

Avoid milk and other dairy products because they may cause digestive problems. Consuming high-fat dairy products may cause diarrhea, painful gas, or cramping for some people after surgery. If you notice bloating or discomfort:

- **Choose low-fat or lactose-free options:** Nowadays, there are plenty of milk and cheese choices that are either low-fat, fat-free, or lactose-free.
- **Experiment with Alternatives:** Almond milk, coconut yogurt, or cashew cheese might become your new favorites.

6) Spices and Sensitivities

While spices add zest to meals, post-gallbladder removal might necessitate a toned-down approach, at least initially.

- **Opt for Mild Over Mighty:** Consider using less spicy and more aromatic herbs like basil, thyme, or rosemary. Some spices, such as cayenne, curry, and cinnamon, can cause upset stomachs. Others, such as ginger and turmeric, are known for their soothing properties.
- **Listen to Your Body:** If a particular food item, even if it's not spicy, causes discomfort, it might be best to avoid it for a while and reintroduce later.

7) Essential Nutrients

The gallbladder, in its role of aiding fat digestion, also indirectly supported the absorption of fat-soluble vitamins. With its removal, there might be challenges in absorbing these nutrients.

- **Vitamins:** Absorption of fat-soluble vitamins, namely A, D, E, and K, may be compromised. It is crucial to incorporate vitamin-rich foods or consider supplementation to prevent deficiencies. Regular check-ups and blood tests can help monitor levels and determine if supplementation is needed.
- **Minerals:** Key minerals, including calcium, magnesium, and zinc, require consistent monitoring. A diet that includes green leafy vegetables, nuts, seeds, and lean proteins can fulfil these mineral needs.

3.2 Nutritional Focus

A. The Importance of Low-Fat Foods

Understanding how to navigate the world of fats is crucial, particularly when you're living without a gallbladder. This chapter describes how high-fat and low-fat foods affect your digestive system, and how to include them in a balanced way. Fats are a more complex macronutrient to break down, especially if you don't have a gallbladder. The less efficient digestion of fats can also interfere with the absorption of fat-soluble vitamins like A, D, E, and K. These vitamins are crucial for a variety of bodily functions, including blood clotting, bone health, and vision. Inadequate absorption can lead to deficiencies, necessitating a more cautious dietary approach.

Let's start by saying that it is not correct to completely eliminate fat from your diet because consuming the appropriate amount of healthy fats can protect against the development of bile acid diarrhea and irritable bowel syndrome (IBS). The ideal amount of fat you should be consuming is between 40g and 50g a day. Saturated fats and trans fats, for example, can lead to inflammation and insulin resistance, making it harder for your body to control blood sugar effectively. To maintain good heart health, go for foods that are rich in omega-3 fatty acids like salmon, olives, avocado, flaxseed, and walnuts.

To manage your fat, cholesterol, carbohydrates, and calorie intake, consider consuming a plant-based diet mostly. This may include vegetables, fruits, and whole grains. Ensure you add lean and low-fat animal-based products such as meat and dairy to your diet in moderate amounts. For good low-fat protein sources, pick tofu, dried beans and peas, low-fat yogurt, low-fat or skim milk, low-fat cheese, and tuna in water.

B. The Importance of Whole Grains

Consuming whole grains may be beneficial for people who have had their gallbladder removed. They help maintain a stable blood sugar level and offer sustained energy, which can be especially beneficial when your body is adjusting to its new digestive landscape. Whole grains are grains that are intact, meaning they include all parts of the grain: the bran, germ, and endosperm. This gives them a high nutrient profile, including:

- **Fiber**: Essential for improving bowel movements and aiding digestion.
- **Vitamins**: Particularly B vitamins (essential for energy metabolism), A and E.
- **Minerals**: Such as iron, magnesium, and zinc.
- **Phytonutrients**: Which have antioxidant properties.

Some examples of common whole grains are:

- **Black, Brown, Red and Wild Rice**: A good substitute for white rice, these other kinds of rice retains its nutrient-rich bran and germ.
- **Quinoa**: Rich in protein and fiber, quinoa is also gluten-free, making it an excellent choice for those with gluten sensitivities.
- **Barley**: it can be an excellent addition to soups and stews.
- **Oats**: Ideal for breakfast, oats are rich in soluble fiber and can help in lowering cholesterol levels.
- **Whole Wheat Bread, Pasta or Crackers**: Opt for bread, pasta or crackers that lists 'whole wheat' as the first ingredient.
- **Millet and Sorghum**: These grains are rich in nutrients and can be used in a variety of dishes, from salads to desserts.

C. The Importance of Fiber

As mentioned above, fiber comes in two main types, soluble and insoluble, each with its own unique benefits:

Soluble Fiber (pectins, gums, mucilagenes): This type dissolves in water and forms a gel-like substance in your intestines. It effectively control the absorption of sugars and fats. This leads to a stabilization of cholesterol levels and blood glucose. In addition, soluble fiber aids digestion, increases the amount of gut bacteria that fight inflammation, and may reduce the risk of heart disease. Legumes and fruit are great sources of these fibers: beans, chickpeas, peas, oats, barley, apples, berries, bananas, pears, prunes and citrus fruits.

Insoluble Fiber (cellulose, hemicellulose, lignin): This fiber type does not dissolve in water or body fluids, but it increases stool volume, aiding with constipation, a common issue after gallbladder removal. It also promotes easier food movement through the intestines, ultimately facilitating the elimination of stool. In addition, insoluble fiber helps the body process waste more effectively and lowers the risk of colorectal diseases such as hemorrhoids and diverticulitis. Insoluble fiber is found in foods such as: whole grains, wheat and oat bran, wholemeal flour, nuts, beans and green beans, cauliflower, carrots, potatoes and spinach.

When the gallbladder is removed, it can be harder for the body to digest fat which may lead to digestive problems like bloating, constipation, or diarrhea. Here's where fiber plays a particularly important role:

Regulation of Bile Flow

Fiber is key to regulating bile flow into the small intestine. High-fiber foods help create voluminous stools which can slow down diarrhea. This can make bowel movements less urgent and more predictable.

Stabilizing Gastrointestinal Transit

Fiber helps move food more efficiently through the digestive system, which can help prevent constipation. This condition is common after surgery due to changes in digestive rhythms.

Control of Blood Sugar Levels

Soluble fiber is very helpful in stabilizing blood sugar levels because it isn't easily absorbed and doesn't contribute to quick sugar spikes. It slows down the absorption of sugar into the bloodstream, essentially acting as a buffer. This controlled release of sugar helps maintain a more stable blood sugar level, reducing the strain on your body's insulin response and aiding in overall digestive health. After meals, your blood sugar, insulin, and triglyceride levels increase. If your body remains in this state over time, chronic conditions such as obesity, diabetes, and heart and brain diseases become more likely. To prevent this, we can eat larger amounts of food that are high in soluble fiber. Both individuals with and without diabetes will experience a decrease in blood sugar and triglyceride levels after the meal.

Fats Absorption

Soluble fiber in food, especially, can link with fats in the digestive system. This can assist in removing some fats and steadying spikes in triglycerides after eating.

D. How to Add Fiber to Your Daily Routine

Starting the Day Right: Breakfast
- **High-Fiber Cereal:** Opt for cereals that list whole grains as the first ingredient and have at least 5 grams of fiber per serving (whole-wheat bran flakes, shredded wheat).
- **Fruit Smoothies:** Blend a smoothie with fibrous fruits like berries or bananas and throw in a spoon of chia seeds or flaxseeds.
- **Oatmeal:** Use rolled oats and add fruits like banana, berries or apple for an extra fiber boost.

Midday Boost: Lunch
- **Whole-Grain Bread:** If you're having a sandwich, make sure it's made with whole-grain bread.
- **Add a Salad:** Incorporate a small salad with lots of greens and crunchy veggies before your main course.
- **Legume-based Soups:** Lentil or chickpea soups are excellent ways to add more fiber.

<u>Snack Time Choices</u>
- **Fruit**: An apple or pear can be an excellent portable snack.
- **Nuts and Seeds**: Almonds, chia, and flaxseeds are good but high in calories, so eat in moderation.
- **Whole-Grain Crackers**: These can be paired with hummus or avocado for added fiber.

<u>Closing the Day: Dinner</u>
- **Brown Rice or Quinoa**: Opt for whole grains over white rice or pasta.
- **Steamed or Roasted Veggies**: These add color, flavor, and most importantly, fiber to your plate.
- **Starchy Foods**: Choose high-fiber starchy foods like sweet potatoes or whole-grain rolls.

It is recommended that you consume 25-35 grams of fiber each day. Drinking plenty of water is necessary to maximize the positive effects of dietary fiber. Since water is closely linked to the action of fiber, insufficient water intake can significantly decrease its benefits, and sometimes even cause the opposite effect. It is recommended to avoid exceeding the indicated dosages to prevent excessive reduction of important nutrients like iron, calcium, zinc, and active drug ingredients.

E. Foods That Create Flatulence

Flatulence can be a sensitive topic but it's an important one to address, especially when you're navigating life without a gallbladder. Certain foods are more likely to produce gas due to their composition of carbohydrates, fiber, and natural gases. Here are some of the top culprits:
- **Beans and Lentils**: High in fiber and complex carbohydrates, these foods can be difficult to break down, producing gas during the fermentation process in the gut.
- **Cabbage, Broccoli, Brussels Sprouts, and Cauliflower**: These cruciferous vegetables contain a complex sugar called raffinose, which the body has difficulty digesting, leading to gas.
- **Carbonated Drinks**: Soda and sparkling water contain carbon dioxide, a natural gas, which can get trapped in the digestive system.
- **Dairy Products**: Lactose, the sugar found in milk and dairy products, can be hard to digest for some people, resulting in gas.
- **Whole Grains**: While excellent for fiber, some whole grains like wheat and bran also contain raffinose, contributing to gas production.
- **Fruits like Apples, Blackberries, Pears, and Watermelon**: These fruits contain both fiber and natural sugars like fructose and sorbitol, which can ferment in the gut and produce gas.
- **Onions and Garlic**: These foods contain fructans, a type of soluble fiber that the gut can find hard to digest, leading to gas.
- **Artificial Sweeteners**: Sorbitol, Xylitol, and Mannitol are often found in sugar-free gum and candies can be hard to digest, causing gas. Those can cause gas or act as a laxative for some individuals.
- **Sugar-alcohol diet beverages**: Sugar-alcohol can aid in weight loss, but excessive consumption can cause a laxative effect. Check labels for ingredients like xylitol and mannitol.
- **Fatty Foods**: High-fat foods can delay stomach emptying, leading to bloating and, in some cases, increased flatulence.

It is necessary to observe reactions to different foods. Understanding the foods that contribute to flatulence can help you make informed choices, particularly when your digestive system is already compromised due to the lack of a gallbladder. You may opt to limit or avoid these foods or consume them in moderation. Always consult your healthcare provider for personalized advice.

SCAN THE QR CODE

SCAN ME

OR COPY AND PASTE THE URL:
http://bit.ly/3Pbo4yJ

Chapter 4: Everyday Recipes

In our bustling lives, finding the right balance between nutrition, taste, and time can be a true culinary challenge. This chapter promises to be your go-to solution, offering a collection of easy, quick, and delicious recipes to brighten up your meal times. Whether you're in the mood for a hearty breakfast, a light salad, a flavorful meat or fish dish, or even a tempting dessert, we've got you covered. And for our vegan and vegetarian friends, there's a special section dedicated just for you. Dive in and discover recipes that will not only satiate your taste buds but also seamlessly fit into your daily routine.

Note: Nutritional values are approximate and may vary based on the specific ingredients used.

4.1 Breakfast Recipes

Quinoa Breakfast Bowl with Fresh Berries

Preparation Time: 10 minutes; Cooking Time: 20 minutes; Serving Size: 2 servings

Ingredients:

- 1 cup quinoa, rinsed
- 2 cups water
- 1 cup fresh mixed berries (strawberries, blueberries, raspberries)
- 1 medium apple, diced
- 1 tablespoon chia seeds
- 1 tablespoon flaxseeds
- 2 cups almond milk or skim milk
- 1 tablespoon honey or maple syrup (optional)

Instructions:

1. **Cook Quinoa:** Place the quinoa and water in a medium saucepan. Bring to a boil, then reduce heat to low, cover, and simmer for about 15 minutes or until the quinoa is cooked and water is absorbed. Fluff with a fork and set aside to cool slightly.
2. **Prepare Fresh Fruits:** While the quinoa is cooking, wash and slice the mixed berries and dice the apple.
3. **Assemble Bowls:** Divide the cooked quinoa between two bowls.
4. **Add Fruits and Seeds:** Top each bowl with a generous portion of mixed berries and diced apple. Sprinkle chia seeds and flaxseeds over the top.
5. **Add Milk and Optional Sweetener:** Pour a cup of almond milk or skim milk over each bowl. If you prefer a sweeter breakfast, drizzle honey or maple syrup over the top.
6. **Serve and Enjoy:** Your Quinoa Breakfast Bowl with Fresh Berries is ready to be enjoyed. Serve immediately for a nutritious start to your day!

Nutritional Facts: Calories: 300 | Carbohydrates: 50g | Protein: 10g | Fat: 6g | Fiber: 8g | Sugar: 10g | Sodium: 50mg | Potassium: 635mg | Calcium: 200mg | Iron: 4mg

Spinach and Mushroom Egg White Scramble

Preparation Time: 10 minutes; Cooking Time: 10 minutes; Serving Size: 2 servings

Ingredients:

- 4 large egg whites
- 2 cups fresh spinach, washed and chopped
- 1 cup mushrooms, sliced
- 1 small onion, finely chopped
- 2 cloves garlic, minced
- 1 teaspoon canola oil
- Salt and pepper to taste
- 2 tablespoons low-fat cheese, shredded (optional)

Instructions:

1. **Prep Ingredients**: Chop the spinach, slice the mushrooms, chop the onion, and mince the garlic. Keep them separate.
2. **Heat the Pan**: Place a non-stick skillet over medium heat and add 1 teaspoon of canola oil.
3. **Cook the Vegetables**: Add the chopped onion and garlic to the skillet and sauté for 2-3 minutes until the onion turns translucent. Add the mushrooms and continue to cook for another 2 minutes.
4. **Add Spinach**: Incorporate the chopped spinach into the skillet and cook for another 2-3 minutes or until the spinach wilts.
5. **Cook the Egg Whites**: In a separate bowl, lightly beat the egg whites with a fork. Pour the beaten egg whites over the vegetables in the skillet. Let it sit for a minute, and then gently stir to combine.
6. **Season and Optional Cheese**: Add salt and pepper to taste. If you're using low-fat cheese, sprinkle it on top of the eggs during the last minute of cooking.
7. **Final Stir and Serve**: Give the scramble one final stir, and then divide it into two servings. Serve immediately, perhaps alongside a side of whole-grain toast if desired.

Nutritional Facts: Calories: 140 | Carbohydrates: 8g | Protein: 14g | Fat: 5g | Saturated Fat: 1g | Cholesterol: 0mg | Sodium: 200mg | Fiber: 2g | Sugar: 4g | Calcium: 150mg | Iron: 2mg

Blueberry Oatmeal Smoothie with Chia Seeds

Preparation Time: 10 minutes; Cooking Time: 0 minutes; Serving Size: 2 servings

Ingredients:

- 1 cup fresh blueberries
- 1 ripe banana, peeled and sliced
- 1/2 cup rolled oats
- 2 cups almond milk or skim milk
- 1 tablespoon chia seeds
- 1 tablespoon honey or maple syrup (optional)
- 1/2 teaspoon vanilla extract (optional)

Instructions:

1. **Prepare Ingredients:** Wash the blueberries and peel and slice the banana. Measure out the oats, chia seeds, and other ingredients.
2. **Blend Base Ingredients:** In a high-speed blender, combine the blueberries, banana, rolled oats, and almond milk or skim milk. Blend on high until smooth.
3. **Add Chia Seeds:** Pause to add the chia seeds to the blended mixture.
4. **Optional Sweeteners and Flavor:** If you'd like your smoothie a bit sweeter, add honey or maple syrup. For added depth of flavor, include vanilla extract. Blend again briefly to mix.
5. **Check Consistency:** If the smoothie is too thick, you can add a bit more almond milk or skim milk and blend again until you reach your desired consistency.
6. **Serve:** Pour the smoothie into two glasses, serve immediately and enjoy!

Nutritional Facts: Calories: 250 | Protein: 8g | Carbohydrates: 45g | Dietary Fiber: 10g | Sugars: 20g | Fat: 4g | Saturated Fat: 0.5g | Sodium: 120mg | Potassium: 450mg

Egg-Free Banana Pancakes

Preparation Time: 10 minutes; Cooking Time: 15 minutes; Serving Size: 2 servings

Ingredients:

- 2 ripe bananas (about 200 g of pulp)
- 80 g whole-grain flour
- 60 g soy milk (or any other vegetable milk)
- 2 teaspoons baking powder
- 1/2 teaspoon ground cinnamon or ginger powder (optional)
- Pinch of salt (optional)
- Fresh berries for garnish (optional)
- Maple syrup for serving (optional, ensure it's 100% pure to avoid added sugars)

Instructions:

1. **Mash the Bananas:** Peel the ripe bananas and place them in a mixing bowl. Use a fork or a potato masher to mash them until smooth.
2. **Dry Ingredients:** In another bowl, combine whole-grain flour, baking powder, and cinnamon or ginger powder, if using. Mix well to combine.
3. **Combine Wet and Dry:** Add the mashed bananas to the dry ingredients. Begin to mix, adding the soy milk a little at a time as you mix, until you have a smooth but slightly thick batter.
4. **Heat the Pan:** Place a non-stick skillet or griddle over medium heat. You can add a tiny bit of oil or use cooking spray if you wish, although it may not be necessary if you're using a good non-stick surface. Once hot, reduce to low heat.
5. **Cook the Pancakes:** Use a 1/4 cup measure to pour the batter into the skillet. Cook each pancake for about 2-3 minutes on one side or until bubbles form on the surface. Flip and cook for another 1-2 minutes on the other side.
6. **Serve:** Place the cooked pancakes on a serving plate. If desired, garnish with fresh berries and a drizzle of pure maple syrup.
7. **Optional:** If you like, you can use cinnamon or ginger for added flavor, but this is optional and should be omitted if you are avoiding cinnamon due to dietary restrictions.

Nutritional Facts: Calories: 250 | Carbohydrates: 45g | Protein: 7g | Fat: 5g | Saturated Fat: 1g | Cholesterol: 93mg | Fiber: 6g | Sugar: 11g | Sodium: 150mg | Potassium: 400mg | Calcium: 75mg | Iron: 2mg

Vegetable Omelette with Dairy-Free Cheese

Preparation Time: 10 minutes; Cooking Time: 10 minutes; Serving Size: 2 servings

Ingredients:

- 4 large egg whites
- 1/2 cup dairy-free cheese (e.g., almond, cashew, or soy-based)
- 1 small zucchini, diced
- 1 small red bell pepper, diced
- 1/2 small onion, finely chopped
- 1 clove garlic, minced
- 1 tablespoon sunflower oil or other low-saturated-fat oil
- Salt and pepper to taste
- Fresh herbs like parsley or chives for garnish (optional)

Instructions:

1. **Prepare Vegetables**: Dice the zucchini, bell pepper, and onion. Mince the garlic.
2. **Cook Vegetables**: Heat 1/2 tablespoon of sunflower oil in a non-stick skillet over medium heat. Add the diced vegetables and minced garlic. Sauté until the vegetables are tender, about 5 minutes. Remove from the skillet and set aside.
3. **Prepare Egg Whites**: In a bowl, whisk the egg whites until slightly frothy. Season with salt and pepper to taste.
4. **Cook Omelette**: Heat the remaining 1/2 tablespoon of sunflower oil in the same skillet over medium heat. Pour in the egg whites and cook for about 1-2 minutes until they start to set around the edges.
5. **Add Fillings**: Sprinkle the cooked vegetables and dairy-free cheese evenly over one half of the omelette.
6. **Fold and Cook**: Carefully fold the other half of the omelette over the fillings. Cook for another 2-3 minutes, or until the omelette is fully set and the dairy-free cheese has melted.
7. **Garnish and Serve**: Slide the omelette onto a plate. Garnish with optional fresh herbs before serving.

Nutritional Facts: Calories: 185 | Carbohydrates: 10g | Protein: 12g | Fat: 10g | Saturated Fat: 2g | Cholesterol: 0mg | Fiber: 2g | Sugar: 6g | Sodium: 410mg | Potassium: 350mg | Calcium: 120mg | Iron: 1mg

Overnight Soaked Millet with Fresh Mango

Preparation Time: 10 minutes (plus overnight soaking); Cooking Time: 20 minutes; Serving Size: 2 servings

Ingredients:

- 1 cup millet, uncooked
- 2 cups water for soaking
- 1 ripe mango, peeled and diced
- 2 1/2 cups low-fat almond milk or another dairy-free milk substitute
- 1 tablespoon chia seeds
- 1 tablespoon honey or maple syrup (optional)
- A pinch of salt

Instructions:

1. **Soak Millet**: The night before, place the millet in a bowl and cover it with 2 cups of water. Allow it to soak overnight.
2. **Drain and Rinse**: In the morning, drain and rinse the soaked millet well.
3. **Cook Millet**: Place the drained millet in a saucepan and add 2 cups of almond milk and a pinch of salt. Bring it to a boil over medium-high heat. Reduce the heat to low and simmer for about 15-20 minutes, stirring occasionally, until the millet is soft and most of the liquid is absorbed.
4. **Prepare Mango**: While the millet is cooking, peel and dice the ripe mango. Set aside.
5. **Mix In Chia Seeds**: Once the millet is done cooking, stir in chia seeds and the remaining 1/2 cup of almond milk. Remove from heat and allow it to cool a little.
6. **Sweeten and Serve**: Divide the cooked millet into two bowls. Top each with diced mango. If desired, drizzle with a tablespoon of honey or maple syrup. Serve warm or at room temperature.

Nutritional Facts: Calories: 320 | Carbohydrates: 65g | Protein: 8g | Fat: 3g | Saturated Fat: 0g | Cholesterol: 0mg | Fiber: 9g | Sugar: 22g (if using honey or maple syrup) | Sodium: 80mg | Potassium: 410mg | Calcium: 280mg | Iron: 1.7mg

Baked Sweet Potato and Black Bean Hash

Preparation Time: 15 minutes; Cooking Time: 40 minutes; Serving Size: 2 servings

Ingredients:

- 2 medium sweet potatoes, peeled and diced
- 1 cup cooked black beans (canned or freshly cooked)
- 1 small onion, finely chopped
- 1 medium bell pepper, diced
- 2 cloves garlic, minced
- 1 teaspoon paprika (avoid if you are sensitive to spices)
- 1 tablespoon canola oil or other low-saturated-fat oil
- Salt to taste
- Fresh parsley for garnish (optional)

Instructions:

1. **Preheat Oven**: Preheat your oven to 400°F (200°C).
2. **Prepare Ingredients**: Peel and dice the sweet potatoes. Drain and rinse the black beans if you are using canned. Finely chop the onion and dice the bell pepper.
3. **Toss Ingredients**: In a large mixing bowl, toss the diced sweet potatoes, black beans, chopped onion, bell pepper, and minced garlic with canola oil. Sprinkle with paprika and salt to taste.
4. **Bake**: Spread the mixture in a single layer on a baking sheet. Place it in the preheated oven for about 35-40 minutes or until the sweet potatoes are tender, stirring halfway through the cooking time for even cooking.
5. **Check for Doneness**: Test a piece of sweet potato to ensure it is cooked through and soft but not mushy.
6. **Serve**: Once done, remove from the oven and allow it to cool for a few minutes. Transfer the hash into serving plates and garnish with fresh parsley if desired.

Nutritional Facts: Calories: 315 | Carbohydrates: 60g | Protein: 9g | Fat: 4g | Saturated Fat: 0.5g | Cholesterol: 0mg | Fiber: 14g | Sugar: 12g | Sodium: 250mg | Potassium: 900mg | Calcium: 60mg | Iron: 3mg

Steel-Cut Oats with Sliced Apple and a Drizzle of Honey

Preparation Time: 5 minutes; Cooking Time: 30 minutes; Serving Size: 2 servings

Ingredients:
- 1 cup steel-cut oats
- 3 cups water
- 1 medium apple, sliced thinly
- 1 tablespoon honey (ensure it's 100% pure)
- 1/2 teaspoon ground cinnamon (optional)
- Pinch of salt (optional)

Instructions:
1. **Boil Water**: In a medium saucepan, bring 3 cups of water to a boil.
2. **Cook Oats**: Add steel-cut oats and a pinch of salt to the boiling water. Reduce the heat to low and simmer for 25-30 minutes, stirring occasionally to prevent sticking.
3. **Prepare Apple**: While the oats are cooking, slice the apple into thin slices.
4. **Check Consistency**: Once the oats have absorbed the water and are cooked, remove from heat.
5. **Serve**: Divide the cooked steel-cut oats into two bowls. Top each with half of the sliced apple.
6. **Drizzle Honey**: Drizzle half a tablespoon of honey over each bowl of oats and apple.
7. **Optional**: If you like, you can add a sprinkle of cinnamon for added flavor, but this is optional and should be omitted if you are avoiding cinnamon due to dietary restrictions.

Nutritional Facts: Calories: 280 | Carbohydrates: 52g | Protein: 9g | Fat: 3.5g | Saturated Fat: 0.5g | Cholesterol: 0mg | Fiber: 8g | Sugar: 17g | Sodium: 10mg | Potassium: 150mg | Calcium: 20mg | Iron: 2mg

Almond Milk Chia Pudding with Fresh Fruit

Preparation Time: 10 minutes; Cooking Time: 0 minutes (Chill time: 3 hours); Serving Size: 2 servings

Ingredients:
- 1 cup unsweetened almond milk
- 3 tablespoons chia seeds
- 1 teaspoon pure vanilla extract
- 1 tablespoon honey or maple syrup (optional)
- 1/2 cup fresh berries (strawberries, blueberries, raspberries, etc.)
- 1/2 small papaya, peeled and chopped

Instructions:
1. **Prepare Chia Mixture**: In a bowl, combine the unsweetened almond milk, chia seeds, and vanilla extract. Stir until well mixed.
2. **Sweeten**: If you prefer a sweeter pudding, add 1 tablespoon of honey or maple syrup. Stir well to combine.
3. **Chill**: Cover the bowl with plastic wrap or a lid and refrigerate for at least 3 hours. The chia seeds will absorb the liquid and create a pudding-like texture.
4. **Prepare Fruit**: While the pudding is chilling, wash and slice the fresh berries and papaya. Keep them refrigerated until ready to serve.
5. **Assemble**: Once the chia pudding has thickened, give it a good stir to break up any clumps. Divide the pudding into two serving bowls.
6. **Top with Fresh Fruit**: Add the sliced banana and fresh berries on top of each serving.
7. **Serve and Enjoy**: The pudding can be eaten immediately or stored in the fridge for up to 2 days.

Nutritional Facts: Calories: 175 | Carbohydrates: 25g | Protein: 5g | Fat: 7g | Fiber: 10g | Sugar: 10g (if sweetened with honey) | Sodium: 85mg | Potassium: 300mg | Calcium: 200mg | Iron: 2mg

4.2 Salad Recipes

Roasted Sweet Potato and Black Bean Salad

Preparation Time: 15 minutes; Cooking Time: 30 minutes; Serving Size: 2 servings

Ingredients:

- 1 large sweet potato, peeled and diced into 1-inch cubes
- 1 can (about 15 oz or 425 g) black beans, drained and rinsed
- 2 cups baby spinach
- 1 medium-sized red bell pepper, diced
- 1 tablespoon canola oil
- Juice of 1 lime
- Salt and pepper to taste
- Fresh cilantro, finely chopped (optional for garnish)

Instructions:

1. **Preheat Oven:** Preheat your oven to 400°F (200°C).
2. **Prepare Sweet Potato:** Toss the sweet potato cubes with half a tablespoon of canola oil, and a pinch each of salt and pepper.
3. **Roast Sweet Potato:** Spread the seasoned sweet potato cubes on a baking sheet lined with parchment paper. Roast for 25-30 minutes or until tender and lightly browned.
4. **Prepare Black Beans:** While the sweet potato is roasting, drain and rinse the black beans.
5. **Assemble Salad:** In a large bowl, combine the roasted sweet potato, black beans, baby spinach, and red bell pepper.
6. **Prepare Dressing:** Whisk together the remaining half tablespoon of canola oil, lime juice, salt, and pepper in a small bowl.
7. **Dress the Salad:** Drizzle the dressing over the salad and toss gently to combine all the ingredients.
8. **Garnish:** Optionally, garnish with finely chopped fresh cilantro.
9. **Serve:** Divide the salad between two bowls and serve immediately.

Nutritional Facts: Calories: 330 | Carbohydrates: 54g | Protein: 12g | Fat: 7g | Saturated Fat: 1g | Cholesterol: 0mg | Fiber: 14g | Sugar: 8g | Sodium: 240mg | Potassium: 1100mg | Calcium: 80mg | Iron: 4mg

Shredded Carrot and Beetroot Salad

Preparation Time: 15 minutes; Cooking Time: 0 minutes; Serving Size: 2 servings

Ingredients:

- 2 large carrots, peeled and shredded
- 1 medium beetroot, peeled and shredded
- 1/4 cup chopped flat-leaf parsley
- 2 tablespoons lemon juice
- 1 tablespoon apple cider vinegar
- 1 teaspoon maple syrup or honey
- 1/4 teaspoon salt
- 1/4 teaspoon black pepper
- 2 tablespoons olive oil
- Optional: 1 tablespoon chia seeds or flaxseeds for added texture and nutrition

Instructions:

1. **Prepare Vegetables**: Peel and shred the carrots and beetroot. Place them in a large mixing bowl.
2. **Add Parsley**: Chop the flat-leaf parsley and add it to the mixing bowl with the shredded vegetables.
3. **Prepare Dressing**: In a small bowl, mix together the lemon juice, apple cider vinegar, maple syrup or honey, salt, and pepper. Whisk until well combined.
4. **Combine Dressing and Oil**: Slowly whisk in the olive oil into the dressing mixture until well incorporated.
5. **Assemble Salad**: Pour the dressing over the shredded vegetables and parsley. Mix well to combine.
6. **Add Seeds**: If using, sprinkle chia seeds or flaxseeds over the salad for added texture and nutrition.
7. **Serve and Enjoy**: The salad is best served immediately but can also be refrigerated for up to 24 hours. The flavors will meld and intensify as it sits.

Nutritional Facts: Calories: 210 | Carbohydrates: 28g | Protein: 3g | Fat: 10g | Saturated Fat: 1g | Cholesterol: 0mg | Fiber: 7g | Sugar: 16g | Sodium: 330mg | Potassium: 450mg | Calcium: 70mg | Iron: 1.5mg

Kale and Quinoa Salad with Lemon-Ginger Yogurt Sauce

Preparation Time: 15 minutes; Cooking Time: 20 minutes; Serving Size: 2 servings

Ingredients:
- 1 cup quinoa, rinsed
- 2 cups water
- 4 cups kale leaves, de-stemmed and chopped
- 1 small red bell pepper, diced
- 1 small carrot, shredded
- 1/4 cup raisins or dried cranberries
- 1/4 cup pumpkin seeds or sunflower seeds

For the Lemon-Ginger Yogurt Sauce:

- 1-inch piece of fresh ginger, grated
- 2 tablespoons fresh lemon juice
- 1/2 cup fat-free yogurt (dairy or non-dairy)
- 1 tablespoon fresh dill, finely chopped
- 1 tablespoon fresh chives, finely chopped
- Salt and pepper to taste

Instructions:

1. **Cook Quinoa**: In a medium saucepan, bring 2 cups of water to a boil. Add the quinoa and a pinch of salt. Reduce heat, cover, and simmer for about 15 minutes, or until the quinoa is cooked and water is absorbed. Fluff with a fork and let it cool.
2. **Prepare Kale**: While the quinoa is cooking, wash the kale leaves and remove the stems. Chop the leaves into bite-sized pieces.
3. **Soften Kale**: Place the chopped kale in a large bowl and massage it with your hands for 2-3 minutes to soften the leaves.
4. **Prepare Veggies**: Dice the red bell pepper and shred the carrot. Add these to the bowl with the kale.
5. **Make Yogurt Sauce**: Combine grated ginger, lemon juice, and yogurt in a bowl. Mix until smooth. Add fresh herbs and season with salt and pepper.
6. **Assemble Salad**: Add the cooked quinoa, raisins, and seeds to the bowl with the kale and vegetables.
7. **Toss and Serve**: Drizzle the yogurt sauce over the salad and toss well to combine. Serve immediately or refrigerate for later use.

Nutritional Facts: Calories: 450 | Carbohydrates: 65g | Protein: 12g | Fat: 17g | Saturated Fat: 2g | Cholesterol: 0mg | Fiber: 9g | Sugar: 10g | Sodium: 350mg | Potassium: 900mg | Calcium: 130mg | Iron: 4mg

Cold Lentil Salad with Steamed Vegetables

Preparation Time: 20 minutes; Cooking Time: 30 minutes; Serving Size: 2 servings

Ingredients:

- 1 cup dried green lentils, rinsed and drained
- 2 cups water
- 1 medium zucchini, diced
- 1 medium carrot, diced
- 1 red bell pepper, diced
- 1/2 small red onion, finely chopped
- Juice of 1 lemon
- 1 tablespoon olive oil
- Salt and pepper to taste

Instructions:

1. **Cook Lentils**: In a medium saucepan, combine the green lentils and water. Bring to a boil, reduce heat, cover, and simmer for 25-30 minutes, or until lentils are tender but not mushy. Drain any excess water and set aside to cool.
2. **Steam Vegetables**: While the lentils are cooking, steam the zucchini, carrot, and red bell pepper until they are tender-crisp, about 5-7 minutes. Remove from heat and set aside.
3. **Prepare Dressing**: In a small bowl, whisk together the lemon juice, olive oil, salt, and pepper.
4. **Combine Ingredients**: In a large bowl, combine the cooked and cooled lentils, steamed vegetables, and finely chopped red onion.
5. **Add Dressing**: Pour the dressing over the lentil and vegetable mixture. Toss well to combine.
6. **Chill and Serve**: Place the salad in the refrigerator for at least 30 minutes to allow the flavors to meld. Serve chilled.

Nutritional Facts: Calories: 280 | Carbohydrates: 40g | Protein: 14g | Fat: 6g | Saturated Fat: 0.5g | Cholesterol: 0mg | Fiber: 16g | Sugar: 7g | Sodium: 110mg | Potassium: 740mg | Calcium: 60mg | Iron: 4mg

Asian-Inspired Edamame and Brown Rice Salad

Preparation Time: 15 minutes; Cooking Time: 45 minutes (mostly for rice); Serving Size: 2 servings

Ingredients:

- 1 cup cooked brown rice
- 1 cup shelled edamame, cooked
- 1 medium carrot, julienned
- 1 small red bell pepper, thinly sliced
- 1/4 cup chopped cilantro
- 1 tablespoon low-sodium soy sauce
- 1 tablespoon rice vinegar
- 1 tablespoon maple syrup
- 1 tablespoon corn oil
- 1 teaspoon fresh ginger, minced
- 1/2 teaspoon garlic powder
- Sesame seeds for garnish (optional)

Instructions:

1. **Cook Brown Rice**: Follow package instructions to cook 1 cup of brown rice. Allow it to cool completely before using it in the salad.
2. **Prepare Edamame**: Boil the shelled edamame for about 5 minutes or until tender. Drain and set aside.
3. **Prepare Vegetables**: Julienne the carrot and thinly slice the red bell pepper. Chop the cilantro finely.
4. **Prepare Dressing**: In a small bowl, whisk together low-sodium soy sauce, rice vinegar, maple syrup, corn oil, minced ginger, and garlic powder until well combined.
5. **Assemble the Salad**: In a large bowl, mix together the cooled brown rice, cooked edamame, julienned carrot, sliced red bell pepper, and chopped cilantro.
6. **Add Dressing**: Pour the dressing over the salad ingredients and mix well to combine.
7. **Garnish and Serve**: Sprinkle sesame seeds over the salad if using. Serve immediately, or refrigerate for later use. The salad will keep well for up to 2 days in the fridge.

Nutritional Facts: Calories: 320 | Carbohydrates: 45g | Protein: 12g | Fat: 10g | Saturated Fat: 1g | Cholesterol: 0mg | Fiber: 7g | Sugar: 8g | Sodium: 400mg | Potassium: 500mg | Calcium: 60mg | Iron: 2.5mg

Tofu and Vegetable Poke Bowl

Preparation Time: 20 minutes; Cooking Time: 10 minutes; Serving Size: 2 servings

Ingredients:

- 1 cup cooked brown rice
- 1 block (about 8 oz or 225 g) extra-firm tofu, drained and cubed
- 1 tablespoon canola oil
- 1 cup diced cucumber
- 1 cup shredded carrots
- 1 cup steamed broccoli florets
- 1 avocado, sliced
- 1 tablespoon low-sodium soy sauce
- 1 teaspoon sesame seeds (optional)
- Salt and pepper to taste

Instructions:

1. **Cook Brown Rice**: If you haven't already, cook 1 cup of brown rice according to package instructions.
2. **Prepare Tofu**: Drain and press the tofu to remove excess moisture. Cut it into cubes.
3. **Cook Tofu**: Heat a skillet over medium heat and add the canola oil. Cook the tofu cubes until they are golden brown on all sides. Remove from heat and set aside.
4. **Prepare Vegetables**: Dice the cucumber, shred the carrots, and steam the broccoli florets. Slice the avocado.
5. **Assemble Bowls**: Divide the cooked brown rice between two bowls. Arrange the tofu, cucumber, carrots, broccoli, and avocado slices over the rice.
6. **Add Flavor**: Drizzle each bowl with low-sodium soy sauce, and sprinkle with sesame seeds if using. Season with salt and pepper to taste.
7. **Serve**: Serve immediately, and enjoy your nutritious poke bowl!

Nutritional Facts: Calories: 450 | Carbohydrates: 45g | Protein: 18g | Fat: 23g | Saturated Fat: 3g | Cholesterol: 0mg | Fiber: 10g | Sugar: 5g | Sodium: 280mg | Potassium: 950mg | Calcium: 100mg | Iron: 3mg

Strawberry and Spinach Salad with Balsamic Reduction

Preparation Time: 15 minutes; Cooking Time: 10 minutes; Serving Size: 2 servings

Ingredients:

- 4 cups fresh baby spinach
- 1 cup fresh strawberries, sliced
- 1/4 cup pecans, chopped
- 1/2 cup balsamic vinegar
- 1 tablespoon honey (optional)
- Salt and pepper to taste

Instructions:

1. **Prepare Balsamic Reduction**: In a small saucepan, bring balsamic vinegar to a gentle boil over low heat. Reduce to a simmer and cook until the liquid has reduced by half and has a syrupy consistency. This will take around 10 minutes. If you prefer a sweeter reduction, you can add a tablespoon of honey during the simmering process.
2. **Cool the Reduction**: Remove the saucepan from heat and let the balsamic reduction cool to room temperature. It will continue to thicken as it cools.
3. **Prepare Spinach and Strawberries**: Wash and pat dry the baby spinach and strawberries. Slice the strawberries and set aside.
4. **Prepare Pecans**: Chop the pecans and set aside.
5. **Assemble the Salad**: In a large bowl, combine the spinach, sliced strawberries, and chopped pecans.
6. **Season**: Sprinkle a pinch of salt and pepper over the salad to enhance the flavors.
7. **Drizzle the Reduction**: Drizzle the balsamic reduction over the assembled salad.
8. **Serve**: Toss the salad gently to combine all the ingredients and coat them with the reduction. Serve immediately.

Nutritional Facts: Calories: 150 | Carbohydrates: 19g | Protein: 4g | Fat: 7g | Saturated Fat: 0.5g | Cholesterol: 0mg | Fiber: 4g | Sugar: 13g | Sodium: 150mg | Potassium: 500mg | Calcium: 100mg | Iron: 2mg

Apple, Celery, and Walnut Salad

Preparation Time: 15 minutes; Cooking Time: 0 minutes; Serving Size: 2 servings

Ingredients:

- 1 large apple, cored and thinly sliced
- 2 stalks of celery, thinly sliced
- 1/4 cup walnuts, roughly chopped
- 1 tablespoon lemon juice
- 1 tablespoon olive oil
- Salt and pepper to taste
- Fresh mint leaves for garnish (optional)

Instructions:

1. **Prepare the Apple and Celery**: Core and thinly slice the apple. Thinly slice the celery stalks as well.
2. **Prepare the Walnuts**: Roughly chop the walnuts.
3. **Make the Dressing**: In a small bowl, whisk together the lemon juice, olive oil, salt, and pepper.
4. **Assemble the Salad**: In a medium-sized bowl, combine the apple slices, celery, and walnuts.
5. **Toss with Dressing**: Drizzle the dressing over the apple, celery, and walnut mixture. Toss gently to combine.
6. **Garnish and Serve**: Optionally, garnish the salad with fresh mint leaves before serving.

Nutritional Facts: Calories: 250 | Carbohydrates: 18g | Protein: 3g | Fat: 20g | Saturated Fat: 2g | Cholesterol: 0mg | Fiber: 4g | Sugar: 12g | Sodium: 80mg | Potassium: 300mg | Calcium: 20mg | Iron: 1mg

4.3 Soup Recipes

Cauliflower Soup with Shrimps

Preparation Time: 10 minutes; Cooking Time: 20 minutes; Serving Size: 2 servings

Ingredients:

- 1 medium cauliflower head, cut into florets
- 4 cups low-sodium vegetable broth
- 1 small onion, chopped
- 2 garlic cloves, minced
- 1 cup diced potatoes
- 1/2 cup diced carrots
- 4 oz (about 115 g) shrimps, peeled and deveined
- 1 teaspoon ground turmeric
- 1 tablespoon sunflower oil
- Salt and pepper to taste
- Fresh parsley for garnish (optional)

Instructions:

1. **Prep Cauliflower**: Wash and cut the cauliflower into small florets.
2. **Sauté Aromatics**: In a large saucepan, heat sunflower oil over medium heat. Add the chopped onion and minced garlic. Sauté until the onion becomes translucent, about 3-5 minutes.
3. **Add Turmeric**: Add ground turmeric to the saucepan and stir well to combine with the onions and garlic.
4. **Cook Cauliflower, Potatoes and Carrots**: Add the cauliflower florets, diced potatoes and carrots to the saucepan. Stir well for a few minutes to coat with the turmeric mixture.
5. **Add Broth**: Pour in the low-sodium vegetable broth. Increase heat to bring to a boil, then lower the heat to maintain a simmer. Cook until the vegetables are tender, approximately 15-20 minutes.
6. **Cook Shrimps**: Place the shrimps in a saucepan. Let them cook for 3 to 4 minutes or until they are well cooked and opaque.
7. **Blend**: Once the vegetables are tender, use an immersion blender to purée the soup until smooth. If you don't have an immersion blender, you can transfer the soup to a regular blender, blend until smooth, and then return it to the pot.
8. **Season and Garnish**: Add salt and pepper to taste, then add the shrimps to the soup. If using, garnish with fresh parsley before serving.

Nutritional Facts: Calories: 200 | Carbohydrates: 25g | Protein: 12g | Fat: 6g | Saturated Fat: 0.6g | Cholesterol: 10mg | Fiber: 5g | Sugar: 6g | Sodium: 210mg | Potassium: 750mg | Calcium: 80mg | Iron: 1.5mg

Ginger and Carrot Pureed Soup

Preparation Time: 10 minutes; Cooking Time: 30 minutes; Serving Size: 2 servings

Ingredients:

- 4 large carrots, peeled and chopped
- 1 small onion, chopped
- 1-inch piece of fresh ginger, peeled and grated
- 4 cups low-sodium vegetable broth
- 1 tablespoon canola oil
- Salt and pepper to taste
- Fresh parsley for garnish (optional)

Instructions:

1. **Prep Vegetables**: Peel and chop the carrots, onion, and ginger. Set aside.
2. **Cook the Base**: In a medium-sized pot, heat canola oil over medium heat. Add the chopped onion and sauté until translucent, about 5 minutes.
3. **Add Carrots and Ginger**: Add the chopped carrots and grated ginger to the pot. Stir well to combine with the onion.
4. **Pour in Broth**: Add the low-sodium vegetable broth to the pot. Bring the mixture to a boil.
5. **Simmer**: Lower the heat to maintain a gentle simmer. Cover the pot and cook until the carrots are tender, about 20-25 minutes.
6. **Blend**: Once the carrots are tender, remove the pot from heat. Use an immersion blender to puree the soup until smooth. Alternatively, you can use a standard blender, blending in batches if necessary.
7. **Season**: Add salt and pepper to taste. If the soup is too thick, you can add a little more vegetable broth to reach your desired consistency.
8. **Garnish and Serve**: Pour the soup into bowls and garnish with fresh parsley if desired. Serve warm.

Nutritional Facts: Calories: 120 | Carbohydrates: 22g | Protein: 2g | Fat: 3g | Saturated Fat: 0.2g | Cholesterol: 0mg | Fiber: 4g | Sugar: 11g | Sodium: 300mg | Potassium: 540mg | Calcium: 50mg | Iron: 0.5mg

Lentil and Spinach Stew

Preparation Time: 15 minutes; Cooking Time: 40 minutes; Serving Size: 2 servings

Ingredients:

- 1 cup green lentils, rinsed and drained
- 4 cups low-sodium vegetable broth
- 1 medium onion, finely chopped
- 2 garlic cloves, minced
- 4 cups fresh spinach, washed and roughly chopped
- 1 tablespoon sunflower oil
- 1/2 teaspoon ground turmeric (optional)
- Salt and pepper to taste
- Fresh parsley for garnish (optional)

Instructions:

1. **Cook Lentils**: In a medium pot, add lentils and 3 cups of low-sodium vegetable broth. Bring to a boil, then reduce to a simmer. Cover and cook for 20-25 minutes, or until lentils are tender but not mushy.
2. **Sauté Vegetables**: While lentils are cooking, heat sunflower oil in a separate pot over medium heat. Add chopped onion and minced garlic, sautéing until the onion becomes translucent, about 5 minutes.
3. **Add Turmeric**: Stir in the ground turmeric to the onion and garlic mixture, cooking for another 1-2 minutes.
4. **Combine with Lentils**: Once the lentils are cooked, add them along with any remaining cooking liquid to the pot with the sautéed onion and garlic.
5. **Add Spinach**: Stir in the chopped spinach and the remaining 1 cup of vegetable broth. Cook for another 5-7 minutes, or until the spinach wilts.
6. **Season**: Add salt and pepper to taste.
7. **Garnish and Serve**: Serve hot, garnished with optional parsley.

Nutritional Facts: Calories: 280 | Carbohydrates: 40g | Protein: 18g | Fat: 5g | Saturated Fat: 0.5g | Cholesterol: 0mg | Fiber: 16g | Sugar: 6g | Sodium: 300mg | Potassium: 800mg | Calcium: 100mg | Iron: 6mg

Tomato Basil Soup with Brown Rice

Preparation Time: 15 minutes; Cooking Time: 35 minutes; Serving Size: 2 servings

Ingredients:

- 1 cup brown rice
- 4 cups low-sodium vegetable broth, divided
- 1 can (about 15 oz or 425 g) diced tomatoes, no salt added
- 1 medium onion, chopped
- 2 garlic cloves, minced
- 1 tablespoon corn oil
- 1/2 cup fresh basil leaves, chopped
- Salt and pepper to taste

Instructions:

1. **Cook Brown Rice**: In a medium saucepan, bring 2 cups of low-sodium vegetable broth to a boil. Add the brown rice, reduce heat to low, cover, and simmer for 30-35 minutes, or until the rice is tender and the liquid is absorbed.
2. **Prepare Soup Base**: While the rice is cooking, heat corn oil in another pot over medium heat. Add chopped onion and minced garlic, sautéing until the onion is translucent, about 5 minutes.
3. **Add Tomatoes**: Stir in the can of diced tomatoes (with their juice) into the pot. Simmer for 10 minutes to allow the flavors to blend.
4. **Add Broth**: Add the remaining 2 cups of low-sodium vegetable broth to the tomato mixture and bring to a simmer.
5. **Infuse Basil**: Add the chopped basil leaves to the soup, simmering for another 5 minutes to allow the basil flavor to infuse the soup.
6. **Combine**: Once the brown rice is cooked, add it to the tomato basil soup, stirring to combine.
7. **Season**: Add salt and pepper to taste.
8. **Serve**: Ladle the soup into bowls and enjoy hot.

Nutritional Facts: Calories: 260 | Carbohydrates: 45g | Protein: 6g | Fat: 5g | Saturated Fat: 0.5g | Cholesterol: 0mg | Fiber: 6g | Sugar: 8g | Sodium: 300mg | Potassium: 650mg | Calcium: 50mg | Iron: 3mg

Roasted Red Pepper and Chickpea Soup

Preparation Time: 15 minutes; Cooking Time: 30 minutes; Serving Size: 2 servings

Ingredients:

- 2 large red bell peppers, roasted and peeled
- 1 can (about 15 oz or 425 g) chickpeas, drained and rinsed
- 4 cups low-sodium vegetable broth
- 1 small onion, diced
- 2 cloves garlic, minced
- 1 teaspoon paprika
- 1 tablespoon corn oil
- Salt and pepper to taste
- Fresh basil leaves for garnish (optional)

Instructions:

1. **Prep Peppers**: Roast the red bell peppers in the oven at 400°F (200°C) for 20-25 minutes until the skin is charred. Remove from the oven, let cool, and then peel off the skin.
2. **Sauté Aromatics**: In a large pot, heat corn oil over medium heat. Add the diced onion and minced garlic. Sauté until the onion is translucent, about 3-5 minutes.
3. **Add Chickpeas**: Stir in the drained and rinsed chickpeas to the pot.
4. **Add Roasted Peppers**: Cut the roasted red bell peppers into strips and add them to the pot.
5. **Add Spices**: Add the paprika and stir well to combine all the ingredients.
6. **Pour in Broth**: Add the low-sodium vegetable broth to the pot. Bring to a boil and then lower the heat to simmer for about 10 minutes.
7. **Blend**: Use an immersion blender to purée the soup until smooth. If you don't have an immersion blender, you can transfer the mixture to a regular blender, blend until smooth, and then return it to the pot.
8. **Season and Garnish**: Add salt and pepper to taste. Garnish with fresh basil leaves if desired before serving.

Nutritional Facts: Calories: 230 | Carbohydrates: 33g | Protein: 8g | Fat: 8g | Saturated Fat: 0.6g | Cholesterol: 0mg | Fiber: 9g | Sugar: 9g | Sodium: 320mg | Potassium: 670mg | Calcium: 80mg | Iron: 2.5mg

Vegetable Barley Soup

Preparation Time: 20 minutes; Cooking Time: 45 minutes; Serving Size: 2 servings

Ingredients:

- 1/2 cup barley, rinsed
- 4 cups low-sodium vegetable broth
- 1 medium carrot, diced
- 1 medium zucchini, diced
- 1 small onion, diced
- 2 cloves garlic, minced
- 1/2 cup green beans, chopped
- 1 tablespoon canola oil
- Salt and pepper to taste
- 1 teaspoon dried thyme
- Fresh parsley for garnish (optional)

Instructions:

1. **Cook Barley**: In a medium pot, bring 2 cups of water to a boil. Add the rinsed barley and simmer for 30-35 minutes, or until tender. Drain any excess water and set aside.
2. **Sauté Aromatics**: In a large pot, heat the canola oil over medium heat. Add the diced onion and minced garlic. Sauté until the onion becomes translucent, about 5 minutes.
3. **Add Vegetables**: Stir in the diced carrot, zucchini, and chopped green beans. Sauté the vegetables for 5-7 minutes, until they begin to soften.
4. **Add Spices**: Sprinkle the dried thyme over the vegetables and stir well.
5. **Pour in Broth**: Add the low-sodium vegetable broth to the pot. Bring the mixture to a boil, then reduce the heat and let it simmer for 10 minutes.
6. **Combine with Barley**: Stir in the cooked barley and continue to simmer for another 5 minutes to allow the flavors to meld.
7. **Season and Garnish**: Add salt and pepper to taste. If desired, garnish with fresh parsley before serving.

Nutritional Facts: Calories: 260 | Carbohydrates: 45g | Protein: 6g | Fat: 7g | Saturated Fat: 0.5g | Cholesterol: 0mg | Fiber: 10g | Sugar: 6g | Sodium: 320mg | Potassium: 580mg | Calcium: 50mg | Iron: 2mg

Mushroom and Leek Clear Soup

Preparation Time: 10 minutes; Cooking Time: 30 minutes; Serving Size: 2 servings

Ingredients:

- 1 cup mushrooms, sliced
- 1 medium leek, cleaned and sliced (white and light green parts only)
- 4 cups low-sodium vegetable broth
- 1 tablespoon sunflower oil
- 1 teaspoon dried thyme
- Salt and pepper to taste
- Fresh parsley for garnish (optional)

Instructions:

1. **Prepare Ingredients**: Clean and slice the mushrooms and leek. Keep the white and light green parts of the leek for the soup.
2. **Sauté Leek**: In a medium pot, heat sunflower oil over medium heat. Add the sliced leek and sauté until it becomes tender and translucent, about 3-5 minutes.
3. **Add Mushrooms**: Add the sliced mushrooms to the pot and sauté until they become tender, another 5-7 minutes.
4. **Pour in Broth**: Add the low-sodium vegetable broth to the pot and bring the mixture to a boil.
5. **Season**: Add dried thyme, and salt and pepper to taste.
6. **Simmer**: Reduce heat and let the soup simmer for 15-20 minutes, allowing the flavors to combine.
7. **Garnish and Serve**: Garnish with fresh parsley if desired before serving.

Nutritional Facts: Calories: 110 | Carbohydrates: 12g | Protein: 2g | Fat: 6g | Saturated Fat: 0.5g | Cholesterol: 0mg | Fiber: 1g | Sugar: 3g | Sodium: 150mg | Potassium: 290mg | Calcium: 25mg | Iron: 1mg

Asian-Style Tofu and Bok Choy Soup

Preparation Time: 15 minutes; Cooking Time: 20 minutes; Serving Size: 2 servings

Ingredients:

- 1 block (about 7 oz or 200 g) firm tofu, drained and cut into small cubes
- 1 bunch of bok choy, washed and separated into leaves
- 4 cups low-sodium vegetable broth
- 2 cloves garlic, minced
- 1-inch piece of fresh ginger, grated
- 2 green onions, chopped (for garnish)
- 1 tablespoon low-sodium soy sauce
- Salt to taste

Instructions:

1. **Prepare Ingredients**: Drain and cube the tofu. Wash and separate the bok choy leaves. Mince the garlic, grate the ginger, and chop the green onions.
2. **Broth Preparation**: In a pot, bring the low-sodium vegetable broth to a simmer over medium heat.
3. **Flavor the Broth**: Add the minced garlic and grated ginger to the simmering broth. Allow it to simmer for about 5 minutes to infuse the flavors.
4. **Add Tofu**: Gently add the cubed tofu into the flavored broth. Simmer for another 5 minutes.
5. **Add Bok Choy**: Incorporate the bok choy leaves into the pot, stirring gently so as not to break the tofu cubes. Continue to simmer for another 5 minutes, or until the bok choy is tender.
6. **Season**: Stir in the low-sodium soy sauce and taste the soup. Add a pinch of salt if needed.
7. **Garnish and Serve**: Once the bok choy is tender and the flavors have melded together, remove the soup from heat. Divide the soup into serving bowls and garnish with chopped green onions before serving.

Nutritional Facts: Calories: 125 | Carbohydrates: 10g | Protein: 12g | Fat: 4g | Saturated Fat: 1g | Cholesterol: 0mg | Fiber: 2g | Sugar: 3g | Sodium: 410mg | Potassium: 680mg | Calcium: 150mg | Iron: 2.5mg

4.4 Meat-based Recipes

Skinless Chicken Stir-Fry with Polenta

Preparation time: 15 minutes; Cooking time: 30 minutes; Serving size: 2 servings

Ingredients:
- 1/2 cup cornmeal
- 2 cups water
- 2 skinless chicken breasts
- 1/2 cup diced tomatoes
- 1 medium carrot, thinly sliced
- 1 small red bell pepper, thinly sliced
- 1 medium zucchini, thinly sliced
- 2 cloves garlic, minced
- 1 tablespoon olive oil
- 1/4 cup low-sodium chicken broth
- 1 tablespoon low-sodium soy sauce
- Salt and black pepper to taste
- Fresh oregano leaves (optional)

Instructions:
1. **Prepare Polenta**: In a saucepan, bring 2 cups of water to a boil. Gradually whisk in cornmeal and continue to cook until thickened. Reduce heat to low and simmer, tossing from time to time, until smooth and fluffy, 15 to 20 minutes.
2. **Prepare Chicken**: season the chicken breasts with salt and black pepper to taste.
3. **Heat Oil**: In a large non-stick skillet or wok, heat the olive oil over medium-high heat.
4. **Sauté Chicken**: Add the chicken to the skillet and cook until no longer pink in the center, about 5-7 minutes. Remove chicken from skillet and set aside.
5. **Cook Vegetables**: In the same skillet, add the garlic, tomatoes, carrots, bell peppers, and zucchini. Stir-fry for about 5 minutes, or until the vegetables are tender but still crisp.
6. **Combine Ingredients**: Return the chicken to the skillet and stir well.
7. **Add Liquid**: Pour in the low-sodium chicken broth and low-sodium soy sauce. Stir to combine and let it simmer for another 2-3 minutes.
8. **Final Touch**: Taste and adjust seasoning if necessary.
9. **Serve**: Spoon the stir-fried chicken over a bed of polenta. If desired, top with oregano leaves.

Nutritional Facts: Calories: 420 | Protein: 36g | Carbohydrates: 49g | Fiber: 4g | Sugars: 6g | Fat: 9g | Saturated Fat: 1g | Cholesterol: 80mg | Sodium: 280mg

Lean Turkey Meatballs with Zucchini Spaghetti

Preparation time: 20 minutes; Cooking time: 30 minutes; Serving size: 2 servings

Ingredients:

- 16 oz (about 450 g) lean ground turkey
- 2 medium zucchinis, spiralized into spaghetti-like strands
- 1 small onion, finely chopped
- 2 cloves garlic, minced
- 1 teaspoon dried basil
- 1 teaspoon dried oregano
- 1 egg white
- Salt and black pepper to taste
- 1 cup low-sodium tomato sauce
- 1 teaspoon corn oil (for cooking)

Instructions:

1. **Preheat Oven:** Preheat your oven to 400°F (200°C).
2. **Prepare Meatballs:** In a bowl, mix the ground turkey, chopped onion, minced garlic, dried basil, dried oregano, and egg white. Add salt and black pepper to taste. Form into small meatballs, each about one inch in diameter.
3. **Cook Meatballs:** Place the meatballs on a baking sheet lined with parchment paper. Bake for about 20-25 minutes, or until fully cooked (internal temperature should reach 165°F or 74°C).
4. **Prepare Sauce:** While the meatballs are baking, heat corn oil in a skillet over medium heat. Add the low-sodium tomato sauce and let it simmer for about 10 minutes.
5. **Prepare Zucchini:** While the sauce is simmering, spiralize the zucchinis into spaghetti-like strands using a spiralizer.
6. **Cook Zucchini:** In a separate pan, sauté the zucchini strands over medium heat for about 3-5 minutes, or until they are tender but not mushy. Season with salt and black pepper.
7. **Combine and Serve:** Once the meatballs are done, add them to the skillet with the tomato sauce and let simmer for 2-3 minutes. Serve the turkey meatballs over the zucchini spaghetti.

Nutritional Facts: Calories: 340 | Protein: 45g | Carbohydrates: 18g | Fiber: 4g | Sugars: 8g | Fat: 11g | Saturated Fat: 2g | Cholesterol: 80mg | Sodium: 310mg

Herb-Roasted Chicken Breasts with Steamed Asparagus

Preparation time: 15 minutes; Cooking time: 25 minutes; Serving size: 2 servings

Ingredients:

- 2 skinless, boneless chicken breasts (around 6 oz or 170 g, each)
- 1 bunch of fresh asparagus, trimmed
- 2 teaspoons of canola oil (for chicken marinade)
- 1 tablespoon lemon juice
- 1 teaspoon dried rosemary
- 1 teaspoon dried thyme
- Salt and black pepper to taste
- 1/4 cup low-sodium chicken broth

Instructions:

1. **Preheat Oven**: Preheat the oven to 400°F (200°C).
2. **Marinate Chicken**: In a bowl, mix together canola oil, lemon juice, rosemary, thyme, salt, and pepper. Place chicken breasts in the marinade and let them sit for at least 10 minutes.
3. **Prepare Asparagus**: While the chicken is marinating, prepare the asparagus by washing and trimming the en ds.
4. **Cook Chicken**: Place the chicken breasts on a baking sheet lined with parchment paper or aluminum foil. Pour the low-sodium chicken broth around the chicken breasts to keep them moist during cooking.
5. **Roast Chicken**: Place the baking sheet in the preheated oven and roast for about 20-25 minutes, or until the internal temperature of the chicken reaches 165°F (74°C).
6. **Steam Asparagus**: While the chicken is roasting, steam the asparagus for about 3-5 minutes, or until tender but still crisp. You can use a steamer or just boil them in a small amount of water in a covered pan.
7. **Serve**: Once the chicken is done, carefully remove it from the oven and let it rest for a few minutes. Serve the chicken breasts alongside the steamed asparagus.

Nutritional Facts: Calories: 230 | Protein: 28g | Carbohydrates: 10g | Fiber: 4g | Sugars: 3g | Fat: 8g | Saturated Fat: 1g | Cholesterol: 75mg | Sodium: 230mg

Grilled Turkey and Pineapple Skewers

Preparation time: 20 minutes; Cooking time: 15 minutes; Serving size: 2 servings

Ingredients:

For Turkey Skewers:

- 16 oz (about 450 g) lean turkey breast, skinless and cut into 1-inch cubes
- 1 cup pineapple chunks, fresh or canned (no added sugar)
- 1 tablespoon canola oil
- Salt and pepper to taste

For Marinade:

- 1/4 cup apple cider vinegar
- 1 tablespoon honey
- 1 teaspoon minced garlic
- 1/4 teaspoon ground ginger
- Salt and pepper to taste

Instructions:

1. **Preparation of Marinade**: In a mixing bowl, combine apple cider vinegar, honey, minced garlic, ground ginger, salt, and pepper. Whisk together until well combined.
2. **Marinate Turkey**: Place the turkey cubes in a resealable plastic bag or shallow dish. Pour the marinade over the turkey, seal the bag or cover the dish, and let it marinate in the refrigerator for at least 1 hour.
3. **Prepare Skewers**: If using wooden skewers, soak them in water for 30 minutes to prevent them from burning.
4. **Assemble Skewers**: Thread alternating pieces of turkey and pineapple onto the skewers.
5. **Preheat Grill**: Preheat your grill to medium-high heat.
6. **Grill Skewers**: Brush the skewers lightly with canola oil. Place the skewers on the grill and cook for about 7-8 minutes per side, or until the turkey is cooked through and reaches an internal temperature of 165°F (74°C).
7. **Serve**: Once done, remove from grill and serve immediately.

Nutritional Facts: Calories: 300 | Protein: 40g | Carbohydrates: 25g | Fiber: 2g | Sugars: 20g | Fat: 5g | Saturated Fat: 1g | Cholesterol: 70mg | Sodium: 250mg

Chicken Fajita Stuffed Bell Peppers

Preparation time: 15 minutes; Cooking time: 35 minutes; Serving size: 2 servings

Ingredients:

- 1 large boneless, skinless chicken breast, thinly sliced
- 2 large bell peppers, any color, halved and seeds removed
- 1 tablespoon sunflower oil
- 1 small onion, thinly sliced
- 1/2 medium zucchini, thinly sliced
- 1/2 teaspoon garlic powder
- Salt and pepper to taste

Instructions:

1. **Preheat Oven**: Preheat your oven to 350°F (175°C).
2. **Prepare Bell Peppers**: Cut the bell peppers in half from top to bottom, remove the seeds and membranes, and set aside.
3. **Cook the Chicken Fajita Filling**: Heat sunflower oil in a non-stick skillet over medium heat. Add the thinly sliced chicken and cook for about 5-7 minutes, or until it turns white and is almost cooked through.
4. **Add Vegetables**: To the skillet, add the sliced onion and zucchini. Season with garlic powder, salt, and pepper. Cook for an additional 5-7 minutes, or until the vegetables are tender and the chicken is fully cooked.
5. **Stuff the Bell Peppers**: Evenly distribute the chicken fajita mixture into the halved bell peppers.
6. **Bake**: Place the stuffed bell peppers in a baking dish and cover with aluminum foil. Bake for 20-25 minutes, or until the bell peppers are tender.
7. **Serve**: Once the bell peppers are tender, remove from the oven and serve immediately.

Nutritional Facts: Calories: 280 | Protein: 28g | Carbohydrates: 17g | Fiber: 4g | Sugars: 10g | Fat: 11g | Saturated Fat: 1g | Cholesterol: 65mg | Sodium: 200mg

Lean Turkey Loaf with Roasted Sweet Potatoes

Preparation time: 20 minutes; Cooking time: 45 minutes; Serving size: 2 servings

Ingredients:

For Turkey Loaf:

- 16 oz (about 450 g) lean ground turkey
- 1/4 cup oats
- 1 medium carrot, grated
- 1 medium onion, finely chopped
- 1 egg white, beaten
- 1/4 cup low-sodium chicken broth
- 1 tablespoon olive oil
- Salt and pepper to taste

For Roasted Sweet Potatoes:

- 2 medium sweet potatoes, peeled and diced
- 1 tablespoon olive oil
- Salt and pepper to taste

Instructions:

1. **Preheat Oven**: Preheat the oven to 375°F (190°C).
2. **Prepare Turkey Loaf**: In a large bowl, combine ground turkey, oats, grated carrot, finely chopped onion, beaten egg white, and chicken broth. Season with salt and pepper, and mix until well combined.
3. **Shape Loaf**: Use your hands to shape the turkey mixture into a loaf, and place it in a baking dish lightly greased with olive oil.
4. **Roast Sweet Potatoes**: Toss the diced sweet potatoes in 1 tablespoon of olive oil, and season with salt and pepper. Spread them on a separate baking sheet.
5. **Cook**: Place both the turkey loaf and sweet potatoes in the preheated oven. Bake the turkey loaf for 40-45 minutes, or until the internal temperature reaches 165°F (75°C). Roast the sweet potatoes for 20-25 minutes, or until tender and slightly caramelized.
6. **Rest and Serve**: Remove the turkey loaf from the oven and let it rest for 5-10 minutes before slicing. Serve with the roasted sweet potatoes on the side.

Nutritional Facts: Calories: 450 | Protein: 40g | Carbohydrates: 50g | Fiber: 8g | Sugars: 12g | Fat: 10g | Saturated Fat: 2g | Cholesterol: 100mg | Sodium: 250mg

Seared Chicken with Sautéed Spinach

Preparation time: 10 minutes; Cooking time: 20 minutes; Serving size: 2 servings

Ingredients:

For Seared Chicken:

- 2 boneless, skinless chicken breasts
- 1/2 tablespoon olive oil
- Salt and pepper to taste

For Sautéed Spinach:

- 4 cups fresh spinach leaves
- 1 clove garlic, minced
- 1 tablespoon olive oil
- Salt and pepper to taste

Instructions:

1. **Preheat the Pan**: Heat a non-stick skillet over medium heat and add 1/2 tablespoon of olive oil for the chicken.
2. **Season Chicken**: Season the boneless, skinless chicken breasts with salt and pepper.
3. **Cook Chicken**: Place the chicken breasts in the skillet and cook for about 6-7 minutes per side, or until the internal temperature reaches 165°F (74°C). Remove from the pan and set aside.
4. **Prepare Spinach**: In the same pan, add another tablespoon of olive oil and the minced garlic. Sauté for about 1 minute until the garlic is fragrant but not burnt.
5. **Cook Spinach**: Add the fresh spinach leaves to the pan. Sauté for 3-4 minutes, or until the spinach has wilted. Season with salt and pepper to taste.
6. **Serve**: Plate the seared chicken breasts and top with the sautéed spinach.

Nutritional Facts: Calories: 280 | Protein: 35g | Carbohydrates: 5g | Fiber: 2g | Sugars: 0g | Fat: 13g | Saturated Fat: 2g | Cholesterol: 85mg | Sodium: 200mg

Balsamic Glazed Chicken and Quinoa Salad

Preparation time: 20 minutes; Cooking time: 30 minutes; Serving size: 2 servings

Ingredients:

- 2 skinless chicken breasts
- 1 cup quinoa
- 2 cups mixed salad greens (e.g., spinach, arugula)
- 1 medium tomato, diced
- 1 medium cucumber, diced
- 2 tablespoons balsamic vinegar
- 1 tablespoon corn oil
- Salt and pepper to taste

For the Balsamic Glaze:

- 1/4 cup balsamic vinegar
- 1 tablespoon honey

Instructions:

1. **Cook Quinoa**: Rinse quinoa under cold water. In a saucepan, bring 2 cups of water to a boil, add the quinoa, reduce heat to low, cover, and cook for 15 minutes. Fluff with a fork and set aside to cool.
2. **Prepare Chicken**: Season chicken breasts with salt and pepper.
3. **Cook Chicken**: Heat corn oil in a non-stick pan over medium heat. Add the chicken and cook until no longer pink in the middle, about 6-7 minutes per side. Remove from heat and let rest for a few minutes before slicing.
4. **Prepare Balsamic Glaze**: In a small saucepan, combine 1/4 cup of balsamic vinegar and honey. Bring to a simmer over low heat and reduce until it thickens into a glaze, about 5-7 minutes. Set aside.
5. **Assemble Salad**: In a large bowl, combine the cooked quinoa, mixed greens, diced tomato, and cucumber.
6. **Add Chicken**: Place the sliced chicken on top of the salad mixture.
7. **Drizzle Balsamic Glaze**: Drizzle the prepared balsamic glaze over the chicken and salad.
8. **Season**: Add a splash of balsamic vinegar, salt, and pepper to the salad for extra flavor.
9. **Serve**: Divide the salad into two portions and serve immediately.

Nutritional Facts: Calories: 500 | Protein: 35g | Carbohydrates: 55g | Fiber: 6g | Sugars: 10g | Fat: 15g | Saturated Fat: 2g | Cholesterol: 75mg | Sodium: 200mg

4.5 Fish-based Recipes

Herb-Crusted Haddock with Steamed Asparagus

Preparation time: 15 minutes; Cooking time: 20 minutes; Serving size: 2 servings

Ingredients:

- 2 haddock fillets (about 6 oz or 170 g, each)
- 1 bunch asparagus, trimmed
- 1 cup whole-grain breadcrumbs
- 1 tablespoon dried parsley
- 1 tablespoon dried thyme
- Salt, to taste
- Freshly ground black pepper, to taste
- 1 tablespoon lemon juice
- 1 tablespoon olive oil

Instructions:

1. **Preheat Oven:** Set your oven to 400°F (200°C) and line a baking sheet with parchment paper.
2. **Prepare Asparagus:** Place the trimmed asparagus spears in a steaming basket over a pot of boiling water. Cover and steam for 4-5 minutes, or until tender but still vibrant green. Remove from heat and set aside.
3. **Make Herb Crust:** In a bowl, combine the whole-grain breadcrumbs, dried parsley, and dried thyme. Season with a pinch of salt and black pepper.
4. **Prep Haddock:** Pat the haddock fillets dry with a paper towel. Drizzle each fillet with lemon juice.
5. **Coat Haddock:** Press the breadcrumb mixture onto the top side of each haddock fillet, making sure it adheres well.
6. **Cook Haddock:** Heat the olive oil in a non-stick, oven-safe skillet over medium-high heat. Carefully place the herb-crusted haddock fillets in the skillet and sear for about 2 minutes or until the crust begins to brown. Transfer the skillet to the preheated oven and bake for 10-12 minutes, or until the fish flakes easily with a fork.
7. **Assemble and Serve:** Place the steamed asparagus on each plate. Lay a haddock fillet beside the asparagus.
8. **Garnish and Serve:** If desired, you can garnish with a lemon wedge or a sprinkle of fresh parsley before serving.

Nutritional Facts: Calories: 350 | Protein: 32g | Carbohydrates: 22g | Fiber: 3g | Sugars: 2g | Fat: 14g | Saturated Fat: 2g | Cholesterol: 80mg | Sodium: 250mg

Baked Tilapia and Veggie Foil Packs

Preparation time: 15 minutes; Cooking time: 20 minutes; Serving size: 2 servings

Ingredients:

- 2 tilapia fillets (about 6 oz or 170 g, each)
- 1 medium zucchini, thinly sliced
- 1 medium yellow squash, thinly sliced
- 1 medium carrot, thinly sliced
- 1 small red onion, thinly sliced
- 1 lemon, thinly sliced
- 2 tablespoons fresh parsley, finely chopped
- Salt and pepper to taste
- 1/4 cup water

Instructions:

1. **Preheat Oven**: Preheat your oven to 400°F (200°C).
2. **Prepare Foil Packs**: Cut two large squares of aluminum foil. Make sure they are large enough to hold half of the vegetables and one tilapia fillet each.
3. **Season Veggies**: In a bowl, mix together the sliced zucchini, yellow squash, carrot, and red onion. Sprinkle a little salt and pepper to taste and toss well.
4. **Assemble Packs**: Divide the seasoned vegetable mixture between the two foil squares. Place a tilapia fillet on top of each pile of veggies.
5. **Add Lemon and Parsley**: Place lemon slices on top of the tilapia fillets. Sprinkle the finely chopped parsley over the top.
6. **Seal and Bake**: Fold the foil over the fish and vegetables, sealing the edges tightly to create a packet. Place the packets on a baking tray and bake for 18-20 minutes.
7. **Check for Doneness**: Carefully open one of the foil packs to check if the fish is cooked through and flakes easily with a fork.
8. **Serve**: Once cooked, carefully open the foil packs (watch out for steam), and serve immediately.

Nutritional Facts: Calories: 210 | Protein: 35g | Carbohydrates: 12g | Fiber: 3g | Sugars: 6g | Fat: 2g | Saturated Fat: 0.4g | Cholesterol: 85mg | Sodium: 120mg

Poached Rainbow Trout with Fresh Herbs

Preparation time: 10 minutes; Cooking time: 15 minutes; Serving size: 2 servings

Ingredients:

- 2 rainbow trout fillets (about 6 oz or 170 g, each)
- 4 cups of water for poaching
- 1/2 teaspoon salt
- 1 bay leaf
- 2 sprigs of fresh thyme
- 2 sprigs of fresh parsley
- 1 lemon, sliced
- Freshly ground black pepper to taste

Instructions:

1. **Prepare Poaching Liquid**: In a large, shallow pan, add 4 cups of water, salt, bay leaf, thyme, and parsley sprigs. Bring the mixture to a gentle simmer over medium heat.
2. **Prepare Fish**: While the water is heating, rinse the rainbow trout fillets and pat them dry with a paper towel.
3. **Poach Fish**: Once the water is simmering, gently lower the trout fillets into the poaching liquid. Add the lemon slices to the liquid around the fish.
4. **Cook**: Let the fish poach for about 7-10 minutes, or until the fillets turn opaque and can easily be flaked with a fork.
5. **Check for Doneness**: Carefully lift a fillet out of the water and check for doneness. If the fish flakes easily, it's ready.
6. **Remove Herbs and Lemon**: Discard the used bay leaf, thyme, parsley, and lemon slices from the poaching liquid.
7. **Serve**: Gently lift the poached trout fillets out of the poaching liquid using a slotted spoon and place them on serving plates. Sprinkle freshly ground black pepper over the top, if desired, and garnish with fresh herbs.

Nutritional Facts: Calories: 232 | Protein: 35g | Carbohydrates: 2g | Fiber: 0.5g | Sugars: 1g | Fat: 9g | Saturated Fat: 2g | Cholesterol: 98mg | Sodium: 635mg

Rosemary and Garlic Cod with Steamed Green Beans

Preparation time: 10 minutes; Cooking time: 15 minutes; Serving size: 2 servings

Ingredients:

- 2 cod fillets (about 6 oz or 170 g, each)
- 2 teaspoons minced garlic
- 2 teaspoons fresh rosemary, finely chopped
- Salt and pepper to taste
- 1/4 cup water (for steaming)
- 8 oz (about 225 g) green beans, ends trimmed

Instructions:

1. **Preheat Oven**: Preheat your oven to 375°F (190°C).
2. **Prepare Cod**: Pat dry the cod fillets with a paper towel. Place them on a baking sheet lined with parchment paper.
3. **Season**: Sprinkle the minced garlic, fresh rosemary, salt, and pepper evenly over the top of each cod fillet.
4. **Bake**: Place the baking sheet in the preheated oven and bake for 12-15 minutes, or until the fish flakes easily when tested with a fork.
5. **Prepare Green Beans**: While the fish is baking, fill a pot with about 1 inch of water and bring to a boil. Place a steamer basket in the pot, making sure the water does not touch the bottom of the basket.
6. **Steam Green Beans**: Place the trimmed green beans in the steamer basket. Cover the pot and steam for about 5-7 minutes, or until the green beans are tender but still crisp.
7. **Check for Doneness**: Carefully remove the cod from the oven and check for doneness. The fish should be opaque and flake easily.
8. **Serve**: Serve the baked cod hot, accompanied by the steamed green beans.

Nutritional Facts: Calories: 210 | Protein: 35g | Carbohydrates: 12g | Fiber: 4g | Sugars: 4g | Fat: 2g | Saturated Fat: 0.5g | Cholesterol: 60mg | Sodium: 120mg

Tuna Steak Salad with Mixed Greens

Preparation time: 15 minutes; Cooking time: 6 minutes; Serving size: 2 servings

Ingredients:

- 2 tuna steaks (about 5 oz or 140 g, each)
- 4 cups mixed greens (e.g., spinach, arugula, romaine)
- 1 medium carrot, thinly sliced
- 1/2 cucumber, thinly sliced
- 10 cherry tomatoes, halved
- Juice of 1 lemon
- 1 ½ tablespoon olive oil
- Salt, to taste
- Freshly ground black pepper, to taste
- 1 teaspoon dried thyme (optional)

Instructions:

1. **Preheat the Grill or Grill Pan**: Preheat your grill or grill pan over medium-high heat.
2. **Prepare Tuna Steaks**: Pat the tuna steaks dry with a paper towel. Lightly brush each side with olive oil and season with salt, black pepper, and optional dried thyme.
3. **Grill Tuna Steaks**: Place the tuna steaks on the grill and cook for 2-3 minutes per side for medium-rare, or longer to your preferred doneness.
4. **Prepare Salad Base**: While the tuna is grilling, in a large bowl, mix the mixed greens, carrot slices, cucumber slices, and cherry tomatoes.
5. **Dress the Salad**: In a small bowl, mix the lemon juice, 1 tablespoon olive oil, salt, and black pepper to make the dressing. Drizzle the dressing over the mixed greens and toss well to combine.
6. **Assemble and Serve**: Once the tuna steaks are done, slice them thinly against the grain. Place the slices on top of the prepared salad and serve immediately.

Nutritional Facts: Calories: 340 | Protein: 40g | Carbohydrates: 12g | Fiber: 3g | Sugars: 6g | Fat: 15g | Saturated Fat: 2g | Cholesterol: 50mg | Sodium: 290mg

Spiced but Not Spicy Catfish with Quinoa

Preparation time: 20 minutes; Cooking time: 20 minutes; Serving size: 2 servings

Ingredients:

- 2 catfish fillets (about 6 oz or 170 g, each)
- 1 cup quinoa, rinsed
- 2 cups low-sodium vegetable broth
- 1 teaspoon paprika (not hot)
- 1 teaspoon garlic powder
- 1 teaspoon onion powder
- Salt, to taste
- Freshly ground black pepper, to taste
- 1 tablespoon olive oil
- Juice of 1/2 lemon
- 2 tablespoons fresh parsley, finely chopped (optional)

Instructions:

1. **Cook Quinoa:** In a medium saucepan, bring the low-sodium vegetable broth to a boil. Add the quinoa, reduce heat to low, cover, and cook for 15 minutes or until quinoa is fluffy and the liquid is absorbed. Fluff with a fork and set aside.
2. **Preheat Oven:** Preheat your oven to 400°F (200°C).
3. **Prepare Catfish:** Pat the catfish fillets dry with a paper towel. In a small bowl, mix together the paprika, garlic powder, and onion powder. Sprinkle the spice mix evenly over both sides of each catfish fillet.
4. **Cook Catfish:** Heat olive oil in a non-stick, oven-safe skillet over medium-high heat. Place the catfish fillets in the skillet and cook for 2-3 minutes on each side until lightly browned. Transfer the skillet to the preheated oven and bake for an additional 5-7 minutes, or until the catfish flakes easily with a fork.
5. **Assemble and Serve:** Divide the cooked quinoa between two plates. Place a catfish fillet on top of each bed of quinoa. Drizzle lemon juice over the catfish and garnish with optional fresh parsley.
6. **Serve Immediately:** Serve your spiced but not spicy catfish and quinoa hot, either as is or with a side of steamed vegetables for added nutrition.

Nutritional Facts: Calories: 540 | Protein: 42g | Carbohydrates: 55g | Fiber: 5g | Sugars: 2g | Fat: 18g | Saturated Fat: 3g | Cholesterol: 80mg | Sodium: 300mg

Steamed Sole with Lemon and Dill

Preparation time: 10 minutes; Cooking time: 12 minutes; Serving size: 2 servings

Ingredients:

- 2 sole fillets (about 6 oz or 170 g, each)
- 1 lemon, thinly sliced
- 1 tablespoon fresh dill, finely chopped
- Salt and pepper to taste
- 1/2 cup water

Instructions:

1. **Preheat Steamer:** Set up a steamer or put a steam rack in a large pot and pour water into the pot, making sure the water level is below the steam rack. Bring the water to a simmer.
2. **Prepare Fish:** Pat the sole fillets dry with a paper towel. Sprinkle both sides with a modest amount of salt and pepper.
3. **Add Lemon and Dill:** Place the lemon slices on top of each sole fillet and sprinkle with the finely chopped dill.
4. **Steam the Sole:** Once the water is simmering, place the prepared sole fillets on the steamer rack. Cover and steam for 10-12 minutes, or until the fish is opaque and flakes easily with a fork.
5. **Check for Doneness:** Carefully open the steamer and check the fish for doneness. If it flakes easily with a fork, it's done. If not, cover and steam for another 1-2 minutes.
6. **Serve:** Carefully remove the sole fillets from the steamer and transfer them to plates. Serve immediately, garnished with extra lemon slices and dill if desired.

Nutritional Facts: Calories: 150 | Protein: 25g | Carbohydrates: 5g | Fiber: 1g | Sugars: 1g | Fat: 2g | Saturated Fat: 0.5g | Cholesterol: 70mg | Sodium: 130mg

Halibut Skewers with Zucchini and Bell Peppers

Preparation time: 20 minutes; Cooking time: 10 minutes; Serving size: 2 servings

Ingredients:

- 2 halibut fillets (about 6 oz or 170 g, each), cut into 1-inch cubes
- 1 medium zucchini, cut into 1-inch pieces
- 1 medium red bell pepper, cut into 1-inch pieces
- 1 medium yellow bell pepper, cut into 1-inch pieces
- 2 tablespoons of olive oil
- Salt, to taste
- Freshly ground black pepper, to taste
- Juice of 1 lemon
- 1 teaspoon dried oregano

Instructions:

1. **Preheat the Grill**: Preheat your grill or grill pan over medium heat.
2. **Prepare Skewers**: If you're using wooden skewers, soak them in water for about 20 minutes to prevent burning.
3. **Marinate the Halibut**: In a shallow dish, combine the halibut cubes, lemon juice, oregano, salt, and black pepper. Let the fish marinate for about 10 minutes.
4. **Assemble the Skewers**: Alternate threading the halibut, zucchini, and bell pepper pieces onto the skewers.
5. **Oil and Season**: Lightly brush the skewers with olive oil and season with a pinch of salt and black pepper.
6. **Grill**: Place the skewers on the preheated grill. Cook for about 4-5 minutes on each side, or until the fish is opaque and flakes easily with a fork.
7. **Serve**: Remove the skewers from the grill and serve immediately. You can also squeeze a little more lemon over the top for added flavor, if desired.

Nutritional Facts: Calories: 320 | Protein: 36g | Carbohydrates: 15g | Fiber: 3g | Sugars: 9g | Fat: 12g | Saturated Fat: 1g | Cholesterol: 55mg | Sodium: 300mg

4.6 Vegan and Vegetarian Recipes

Zucchini Noodles with Sun-Dried Tomato Pesto

Preparation time: 15 minutes; Cooking time: 5 minutes; Serving size: 2 servings

Ingredients:

For Zucchini Noodles:

- 2 medium-sized zucchinis, spiralized into noodles

For Sun-Dried Tomato Pesto:

- 1/2 cup sun-dried tomatoes (not oil-packed)
- 1/4 cup fresh basil leaves
- 1/4 cup fresh parsley
- 1 garlic clove
- 2 tablespoons olive oil
- Salt and pepper to taste

Optional Toppings:

- Fresh basil leaves, for garnish

Instructions:

1. **Prepare Zucchini Noodles**: Spiralize the zucchini into noodles and set aside.
2. **Make Sun-Dried Tomato Pesto**: In a food processor, combine sun-dried tomatoes, basil leaves, parsley, garlic, and olive oil. Pulse until a smooth paste forms. Season with salt and pepper to taste.
3. **Cook Zucchini Noodles**: Heat a non-stick skillet over medium heat. Add the zucchini noodles and cook for about 2-3 minutes, just until tender. Remove from heat.
4. **Combine and Serve**: Toss the cooked zucchini noodles with the sun-dried tomato pesto until well combined.
5. **Garnish and Serve**: Divide the noodles between two plates, garnish with fresh basil leaves if desired, and serve immediately.

Nutritional Facts: Calories: 210 | Protein: 6g | Carbohydrates: 17g | Fiber: 5g | Sugars: 9g | Fat: 15g | Saturated Fat: 1g | Cholesterol: 0mg | Sodium: 20mg

Garlic-Free Chickpea and Spinach Curry

Preparation time: 10 minutes; Cooking time: 20 minutes; Serving size: 2 servings

Ingredients:

- 1 can (about 15 oz or 425 g) chickpeas, drained and rinsed
- 2 cups fresh spinach, washed and roughly chopped
- 1 medium onion, finely chopped
- 1 tablespoon sunflower oil
- 1 teaspoon ground cumin
- 1 teaspoon ground coriander
- 1 teaspoon turmeric
- Salt, to taste
- 1 cup low-fat coconut milk
- Fresh cilantro leaves for garnish (optional)

Instructions:

1. **Sauté Onions**: Heat sunflower oil in a non-stick skillet over medium heat. Add the chopped onions and sauté until translucent, about 3-4 minutes.
2. **Add Spices**: Add ground cumin, ground coriander, and turmeric to the onions. Stir well to combine, making sure the onions are well-coated with the spices.
3. **Add Chickpeas**: Incorporate the drained and rinsed chickpeas into the skillet. Stir to mix them with the onions and spices.
4. **Simmer**: Pour in the low-fat coconut milk and stir to combine all ingredients. Bring the mixture to a low simmer, allowing it to cook for about 10 minutes.
5. **Add Spinach**: Fold in the fresh spinach, and let it wilt into the mixture, which should take about 2-3 minutes.
6. **Adjust Seasoning**: Taste the curry and adjust the salt according to your preference.
7. **Garnish and Serve**: If desired, garnish with fresh cilantro leaves before serving.

Nutritional Facts: Calories: 350 | Protein: 12g | Carbohydrates: 45g | Fiber: 11g | Sugars: 9g | Fat: 15g | Saturated Fat: 5g | Cholesterol: 0mg | Sodium: 300mg

Cream-Free Mushroom and Asparagus Risotto

Preparation time: 15 minutes; Cooking time: 40 minutes; Serving size: 2 servings

Ingredients:

- 1 cup Arborio rice
- 1 tablespoon corn oil
- 1 small onion, finely chopped
- 2 cloves garlic, minced
- 8 oz (about 225 g) mushrooms, sliced
- 8 asparagus spears, cut into 1-inch pieces
- 4 cups low-sodium vegetable broth, warm
- Juice of 1 lemon
- Salt and pepper to taste
- Fresh parsley, chopped (for garnish)

Instructions:

1. **Preheat a Pan**: Place a medium-sized non-stick pan over medium heat and add the corn oil.
2. **Sauté Onions and Garlic**: Add the chopped onions and garlic to the pan. Sauté until the onions become translucent.
3. **Cook the Mushrooms**: Add the sliced mushrooms to the pan and sauté until they are soft and their liquid has evaporated.
4. **Add Arborio Rice**: Add the Arborio rice to the pan and stir well, making sure the rice is well-coated with the oil and vegetables.
5. **Start Cooking the Risotto**: Add a cup of warm vegetable broth to the rice and stir constantly until most of the liquid is absorbed.
6. **Add Asparagus and More Broth**: Add the cut asparagus spears to the pan. Continue to add the remaining vegetable broth, one cup at a time, stirring constantly and allowing each addition to absorb before adding the next.
7. **Check for Doneness**: The risotto is done when the rice is tender but still has a bit of a bite, and the mixture is creamy. This will take approximately 30–35 minutes.
8. **Season and Serve**: Remove from heat, add the lemon juice, salt, and pepper to taste. Garnish with fresh parsley before serving.

Nutritional Facts: Calories: 420 | Protein: 10g | Carbohydrates: 82g | Fiber: 4g | Sugars: 6g | Fat: 6g | Saturated Fat: 0.5g | Cholesterol: 0mg | Sodium: 400m

Black Bean Tacos with Cabbage Slaw

Preparation time: 20 minutes; Cooking time: 10 minutes; Serving size: 2 servings

Ingredients:

For the Black Beans:

- 1 can (about 15 oz or 425 g) black beans, drained and rinsed
- 1 teaspoon sunflower oil
- Salt to taste

For the Cabbage Slaw:

- 2 cups shredded green cabbage
- 1 medium carrot, grated
- 1 tablespoon apple cider vinegar
- Salt and pepper to taste

For the Tacos:

- 4 small whole-grain corn tortillas

Optional Toppings:

- Fresh cilantro, chopped
- Lime wedges for serving

Instructions:

1. **Prepare the Black Beans:** In a small pan, heat the sunflower oil over medium heat. Add the drained and rinsed black beans, season with salt, and cook for about 5 minutes, stirring occasionally. Remove from heat and set aside.
2. **Make the Cabbage Slaw:** In a bowl, combine the shredded cabbage, grated carrot, apple cider vinegar, salt, and pepper. Toss well and set aside to let the flavors meld.
3. **Warm the Tortillas:** Place the corn tortillas in a dry skillet over medium heat for about 30 seconds on each side or until they become pliable.
4. **Assemble the Tacos:** Divide the cooked black beans among the 4 warmed tortillas. Top each with a generous serving of cabbage slaw.
5. **Garnish and Serve:** Add fresh cilantro and lime wedges, if desired. Serve immediately.

Nutritional Facts: Calories: 320 | Protein: 12g | Carbohydrates: 60g | Fiber: 15g | Sugars: 5g | Fat: 5g | Saturated Fat: 0.5g | Cholesterol: 0mg | Sodium: 300mg

Stuffed Acorn Squash with Wild Rice and Pecans

Preparation time: 15 minutes; Cooking time: 50 minutes; Serving size: 2 servings

Ingredients:

For the Acorn Squash:

- 1 acorn squash, halved and seeds removed
- 1 tablespoon sunflower oil
- Salt and pepper to taste

For the Wild Rice and Pecan Stuffing:

- 1/2 cup wild rice, uncooked
- 1 1/2 cups low-sodium vegetable broth
- 1/4 cup pecans, chopped
- 1/4 cup dried cranberries
- 1/4 cup chopped parsley
- Salt and pepper to taste

Instructions:

1. **Preheat the Oven:** Preheat your oven to 375°F (190°C).
2. **Prepare the Squash:** Rub the cut sides of the acorn squash with canola oil, and season with salt and pepper. Place the squash cut-side down on a baking sheet.
3. **Roast the Squash:** Bake the squash for about 30-35 minutes, or until tender.
4. **Cook the Wild Rice:** While the squash is roasting, cook the wild rice according to package instructions using low-sodium vegetable broth instead of water.
5. **Prepare the Stuffing:** In a mixing bowl, combine the cooked wild rice, chopped pecans, dried cranberries, and parsley. Season with salt and pepper.
6. **Stuff the Squash:** Once the acorn squash is cooked, flip them so that the cut sides are facing up. Fill each half with the wild rice and pecan stuffing.
7. **Final Roast:** Return the stuffed squash to the oven and bake for an additional 15 minutes.
8. **Serve:** Carefully remove from the oven and let cool for a few minutes before serving.

Nutritional Facts: Calories: 430 | Protein: 8g | Carbohydrates: 61g | Fiber: 8g | Sugars: 14g | Fat: 20g | Saturated Fat: 2g | Cholesterol: 0mg | Sodium: 150mg

Tempeh and Brown Rice Stir-fry with Steamed Veggies

Preparation time: 20 minutes; Cooking time: 30 minutes; Serving size: 2 servings

Ingredients:

For the Stir-fry:

- 1 cup cooked brown rice
- 8 oz (about 225 g) tempeh, cut into cubes
- 1 medium bell pepper, thinly sliced
- 1 small onion, thinly sliced
- 1 tablespoon sunflower oil

For the Sauce:

- 2 tablespoons low-sodium soy sauce
- 1 tablespoon apple cider vinegar
- 1 teaspoon maple syrup or honey
- 1 teaspoon grated fresh ginger

For the Steamed Veggies:

- 1 cup broccoli florets
- 1 cup carrot slices

Instructions:

1. **Prepare the Brown Rice**: If you haven't already, cook the brown rice according to package instructions.
2. **Steam the Veggies**: In a steamer or a pot with a steaming basket, steam the broccoli and carrot slices for about 5-7 minutes or until tender but not mushy.
3. **Prepare the Sauce**: In a small bowl, mix together the low-sodium soy sauce, apple cider vinegar, maple syrup, and grated ginger. Set aside.
4. **Cook the Tempeh**: In a non-stick pan, heat sunflower oil over medium heat. Add the tempeh cubes and sauté for about 5-7 minutes, turning occasionally, until all sides are golden brown.
5. **Add the Veggies**: Add the sliced bell pepper and onion to the pan. Stir-fry for about 3-4 minutes or until the vegetables are slightly tender.
6. **Combine and Cook**: Add the cooked brown rice to the pan with tempeh and vegetables. Pour the sauce over the top and mix well to combine. Cook for another 2-3 minutes.
7. **Serve**: Divide the stir-fry into two portions and serve with the steamed veggies on the side.

Nutritional Facts: Calories: 390 | Protein: 21g | Carbohydrates: 50g | Fiber: 7g | Sugars: 9g | Fat: 13g | Saturated Fat: 2g | Cholesterol: 0mg | Sodium: 390mg

Grilled Portobello Mushrooms with Balsamic Glaze

Preparation time: 15 minutes; Cooking time: 15 minutes; Serving size: 2 servings

Ingredients:
- 4 medium-sized Portobello mushrooms, stems removed
- 1 tablespoon corn oil
- 1/4 cup balsamic vinegar
- 1 tablespoon maple syrup or honey
- A handful of fresh basil leaves, chopped (optional)
- 1 teaspoon sesame seeds (optional)

Instructions:
1. **Preheat the Grill**: Preheat your grill to medium-high heat.
2. **Prepare the Mushrooms**: Brush the Portobello mushrooms lightly with corn oil on both sides.
3. **Make the Balsamic Glaze**: In a small saucepan, combine the balsamic vinegar and maple syrup. Simmer over low heat for 5-7 minutes until it thickens into a glaze.
4. **Grill the Mushrooms**: Place the prepared mushrooms on the grill, gill side up. Grill for about 5-7 minutes on each side or until tender and slightly charred.
5. **Apply the Glaze**: During the last 2 minutes of grilling, brush the mushrooms with the balsamic glaze, making sure to coat them evenly.
6. **Garnish and Serve**: Once done, remove the mushrooms from the grill and garnish with chopped basil and sesame seeds, if using. Serve immediately.

Nutritional Facts: Calories: 140 | Protein: 3g | Carbohydrates: 18g | Fiber: 2g | Sugars: 14g | Fat: 7g | Saturated Fat: 0.5g | Cholesterol: 0mg | Sodium: 20mg

Avocado-Free Guacamole with Peas

Preparation time: 10 minutes; Cooking time: 0 minutes; Serving size: 2 servings

Ingredients:
- 1 cup frozen green peas, thawed
- 1 small tomato, diced
- 1/4 red onion, finely chopped
- 1 clove garlic, minced
- Juice of 1 lime
- 1 tablespoon chopped fresh cilantro
- Salt and pepper to taste

Instructions:
1. **Prepare the Peas**: Place the thawed green peas in a food processor and pulse until you get a smooth, guacamole-like consistency. If you don't have a food processor, you can mash them with a fork or potato masher.
2. **Combine Ingredients**: In a medium-sized mixing bowl, combine the mashed peas, diced tomato, chopped red onion, minced garlic, lime juice, and cilantro.
3. **Season**: Add salt and pepper to taste. Mix well to combine all the ingredients.
4. **Chill**: While this step is optional, chilling the guacamole in the fridge for about 20-30 minutes can help the flavors meld together.
5. **Serve**: Serve the avocado-free guacamole with whole-grain tortilla chips or fresh vegetable sticks like carrots and cucumbers.

Nutritional Facts: Calories: 110 | Protein: 5g | Carbohydrates: 20g | Fiber: 7g | Sugars: 9g | Fat: 1g | Saturated Fat: 0g | Cholesterol: 0mg | Sodium: 20mg

4.7 Dressings and Condiments

Herb-Infused Apple Cider Vinegar Dressing

Preparation time: 5 minutes; Cooking time: 0 minutes; Serving size: 2 servings

Ingredients:

- 3 tablespoons apple cider vinegar
- 1 tablespoon olive oil
- 1 teaspoon honey or maple syrup
- 1 small garlic clove, minced
- 1/4 teaspoon dried thyme
- 1/4 teaspoon dried oregano
- 1/4 teaspoon dried basil
- Salt and pepper to taste

Instructions:

1. **Mix Vinegar and Sweetener**: In a small bowl, combine the apple cider vinegar and honey or maple syrup.
2. **Add Oil**: Slowly whisk in the olive oil to form an emulsion.
3. **Incorporate Herbs and Garlic**: Add the minced garlic, dried thyme, dried oregano, and dried basil to the bowl.
4. **Season**: Add salt and pepper according to your taste preference.
5. **Whisk and Combine**: Whisk all the ingredients thoroughly until well combined.
6. **Taste and Adjust**: Taste the dressing and adjust the seasoning if needed.
7. **Store or Serve**: You can use the dressing immediately or store it in an airtight container in the refrigerator for up to one week. Shake well before using.

Nutritional Facts: Calories: 80 | Protein: 0g | Carbohydrates: 4g | Fiber: 0g | Sugars: 3g | Fat: 7g | Saturated Fat: 0.5g | Cholesterol: 0mg | Sodium: 50mg

Nut-Free Pesto with Basil and Spinach

Preparation time: 10 minutes; Cooking time: 0 minutes; Serving size: 2 servings

Ingredients:

- 1 cup fresh basil leaves, tightly packed
- 1 cup fresh spinach leaves, tightly packed
- 2 cloves garlic
- 1/4 cup grated low-fat Parmesan cheese
- 2 tablespoons lemon juice
- 2 tablespoons water
- A pinch of salt
- A pinch of black pepper

Instructions:

1. **Prepare Ingredients**: Wash the basil and spinach leaves thoroughly. Peel the garlic cloves.
2. **Blend Greens**: In a food processor, combine the basil and spinach leaves. Pulse until finely chopped.
3. **Add Garlic**: Add the garlic cloves to the food processor and pulse again until everything is well combined.
4. **Add Cheese**: Add the grated low-fat Parmesan cheese to the mixture and pulse to combine.
5. **Add Liquids**: Add the lemon juice and water to the food processor. Blend until the mixture becomes a smooth paste.
6. **Season**: Add a pinch of salt and black pepper to taste. Blend once more to mix in the seasoning.
7. **Taste and Adjust**: Taste the pesto and adjust the seasoning, if necessary.
8. **Serve or Store**: You can use the pesto immediately or store it in an airtight container in the refrigerator for up to 3 days.

Nutritional Facts: Calories: 45 | Protein: 4g | Carbohydrates: 4g | Fiber: 1g | Sugars: 1g | Fat: 2g | Saturated Fat: 0.5g | Cholesterol: 4mg | Sodium: 150mg

Sweet Mango Chutney

Preparation time: 10 minutes; Cooking time: 20 minutes; Serving size: 2 servings

Ingredients:

- 1 large ripe mango, peeled and diced
- 1/2 cup apple cider vinegar
- 1/4 cup water
- 1 tablespoon lemon juice
- 2 tablespoons maple syrup (or honey)
- 1/2 teaspoon ground ginger
- 1/4 teaspoon ground cardamom
- 1/2 small red onion, finely diced
- Salt to taste

Instructions:

1. **Prep the Mango**: Peel and dice the ripe mango, making sure to remove the pit.
2. **Cook the Onion**: In a small saucepan over low heat, add the finely diced red onion with 1/4 cup of water and cook until softened, about 5 minutes.
3. **Add Mango and Liquids**: Add the diced mango to the saucepan. Pour in the apple cider vinegar, lemon juice, and water.
4. **Add Sweetener and Spices**: Stir in the maple syrup or honey, ground ginger, and ground cardamom.
5. **Simmer**: Bring the mixture to a simmer over medium heat. Reduce heat to low and continue to simmer, stirring occasionally, for 15 minutes or until the mango softens and the mixture thickens.
6. **Season**: Add a pinch of salt to taste.
7. **Cool and Serve**: Remove the chutney from heat and let it cool down to room temperature before serving. It can be stored in an airtight container in the refrigerator for up to one week.

Nutritional Facts: Calories: 110 | Protein: 1g | Carbohydrates: 26g | Fiber: 2g | Sugars: 23g | Fat: 0g | Saturated Fat: 0g | Cholesterol: 0mg | Sodium: 50mg

Balsamic and Orange Zest Glaze

Preparation time: 5 minutes; Cooking time: 10 minutes; Serving size: 2 servings

Ingredients:

- 1/2 cup balsamic vinegar
- Zest of 1 orange
- 1 tablespoon honey or maple syrup
- Salt to taste
- A pinch of black pepper

Instructions:

1. **Prepare Ingredients**: Measure out all the ingredients and set them aside.
2. **Zest the Orange**: Zest 1 orange carefully, avoiding the bitter white pith. Set the zest aside.
3. **Heat Vinegar**: In a small saucepan over low heat, add the balsamic vinegar.
4. **Simmer**: Allow the vinegar to simmer gently, , until it is reduced by about half.
5. **Add Sweetener**: Stir in the honey or maple syrup.
6. **Add Orange Zest**: Incorporate the orange zest into the simmering mixture. Stir well.
7. **Season**: Add a pinch of salt and black pepper to taste.
8. **Check Consistency**: Continue to simmer until the glaze is thick enough to coat the back of a spoon.
9. **Cool Down**: Remove the saucepan from heat and let the glaze cool.
10. **Serve**: Drizzle over grilled vegetables, fish, or chicken for a flavorful addition to your meal.

Nutritional Facts: Calories: 60 | Protein: 0.3g | Carbohydrates: 14g | Fiber: 0g | Sugars: 12g | Fat: 0g | Saturated Fat: 0g | Cholesterol: 0mg | Sodium: 10mg

Maple-Mustard Dressing

Preparation time: 5 minutes; Cooking time: 0 minutes; Serving size: 2 servings

Ingredients:

- 2 tablespoons Dijon mustard
- 2 tablespoons maple syrup
- 2 tablespoons apple cider vinegar
- A pinch of salt
- A pinch of black pepper

Instructions:

1. **Gather Ingredients**: Ensure you have all your ingredients ready.
2. **Combine Mustard and Maple Syrup**: In a small bowl, combine the Dijon mustard and maple syrup.
3. **Add Vinegar**: Stir in the apple cider vinegar.
4. **Season**: Add a pinch of salt and black pepper to taste.
5. **Whisk**: Use a small whisk or fork to mix everything together until well combined.
6. **Taste and Adjust**: Taste the dressing and adjust seasoning if necessary.
7. **Serve or Store**: The dressing can be used immediately or stored in an airtight container in the refrigerator for up to 5 days.

Nutritional Facts: Calories: 60 | Protein: 0.6g | Carbohydrates: 14g | Fiber: 0g | Sugars: 12g | Fat: 0.4g | Saturated Fat: 0g | Cholesterol: 0mg | Sodium: 110mg

Low-Fat Cucumber and Dill Yogurt Dip

Preparation time: 10 minutes; Cooking time: 0 minutes; Serving size: 2 servings

Ingredients:

- 1 cup low-fat Greek yogurt
- 1/2 cucumber, finely diced
- 1 tablespoon fresh dill, finely chopped
- 1 small clove garlic, minced (optional)
- Juice of 1/2 lemon
- Salt to taste
- A dash of black pepper

Instructions:

1. **Prepare Cucumber**: Wash and finely dice half a cucumber.
2. **Chop Dill**: Finely chop fresh dill to measure about 1 tablespoon.
3. **Mix Yogurt and Lemon Juice**: In a mixing bowl, combine the low-fat Greek yogurt with the juice of half a lemon. Stir until well blended.
4. **Add Herbs and Garlic**: Add the chopped dill and minced garlic (if using) to the yogurt mixture. Stir to combine.
5. **Add Cucumber**: Incorporate the finely diced cucumber into the yogurt mixture.
6. **Season**: Add salt and a dash of black pepper according to your taste preference. Stir the dip until all the ingredients are well combined.
7. **Chill or Serve**: The dip can be served immediately or chilled in the refrigerator for about 30 minutes to let the flavors meld together.
8. **Serve**: Enjoy your low-fat cucumber and dill yogurt dip with sliced veggies or as a spread on whole-grain bread.

Nutritional Facts: Calories: 60 | Protein: 8g | Carbohydrates: 6g | Fiber: 0.5g | Sugars: 4g | Fat: 0.5g | Saturated Fat: 0g | Cholesterol: 5mg | Sodium: 150mg

Stevia-Sweetened Ketchup

Preparation time: 5 minutes; Cooking time: 20 minutes; Serving size: 2 servings

Ingredients:

- 1 cup canned no-salt-added tomato sauce
- 2 tablespoons apple cider vinegar
- 1/4 teaspoon onion powder
- 1/4 teaspoon garlic powder
- 1/8 teaspoon ground allspice
- 1/8 teaspoon ground cloves
- 2-3 drops liquid stevia, or to taste
- Salt to taste

Instructions:

1. **Combine Ingredients**: In a small saucepan, combine the tomato sauce, apple cider vinegar, onion powder, garlic powder, ground allspice, and ground cloves.
2. **Heat Mixture**: Place the saucepan on the stove over low heat.
3. **Simmer**: Let the mixture simmer for about 15-20 minutes, stirring occasionally. This will allow the flavors to meld together.
4. **Add Stevia**: After the simmering time is up, add 2-3 drops of liquid stevia, stirring to combine. Taste and adjust the sweetness as needed.
5. **Season**: Add salt to taste, if needed.
6. **Cool and Serve**: Remove the saucepan from heat and let the ketchup cool to room temperature. Once cool, transfer it to an airtight container.
7. **Store**: Store the ketchup in the refrigerator for up to one week. Shake or stir before using.

Nutritional Facts: Calories: 30 | Protein: 1g | Carbohydrates: 7g | Fiber: 2g | Sugars: 5g | Fat: 0g | Saturated Fat: 0g | Cholesterol: 0mg | Sodium: 15mg

Mint and Pineapple Salsa

Preparation time: 15 minutes; Cooking time: 0 minutes; Serving size: 2 servings

Ingredients:

- 1 cup fresh pineapple, diced
- 1/4 cup fresh mint leaves, finely chopped
- 1/2 small red onion, finely diced
- 1 small cucumber, peeled and diced
- 1 tablespoon lime juice
- Salt to taste
- Freshly ground black pepper to taste

Instructions:

1. **Prepare the Ingredients**: Peel and dice the pineapple and cucumber. Finely dice the red onion and chop the mint leaves.
2. **Combine Fruits and Veggies**: In a medium-sized mixing bowl, combine the diced pineapple, cucumber, and red onion.
3. **Add Herbs**: Add the finely chopped mint leaves to the bowl.
4. **Add Lime Juice**: Drizzle lime juice over the mixture for added flavor and to help keep the fruits and vegetables fresh.
5. **Season**: Add a pinch of salt and freshly ground black pepper to taste.
6. **Mix Well**: Toss all the ingredients together until well mixed.
7. **Taste and Adjust**: Give the salsa a taste and adjust the seasoning, if necessary.
8. **Serve or Store**: You can serve the salsa immediately or let it sit for about 15–30 minutes to allow the flavors to meld together. You can also store it in an airtight container in the fridge for up to 2 days.

Nutritional Facts: Calories: 60 | Protein: 1g | Carbohydrates: 15g | Fiber: 2g | Sugars: 12g | Fat: 0g | Saturated Fat: 0g | Cholesterol: 0mg | Sodium: 50mg

4.8 Snacks and Appetizers

Zucchini and Carrot Fritters (Oil-Free)

Preparation time: 15 minutes; Cooking time: 25 minutes; Serving size: 2 servings

Ingredients:

- 2 small zucchinis, grated
- 2 small carrots, grated
- 1 egg, beaten
- 1/4 cup oat flour
- 1/4 teaspoon salt (optional)
- 1/4 teaspoon black pepper (adjust according to tolerance)
- 1/2 teaspoon dried thyme
- 1/4 cup low-fat grated parmesan cheese
- Canola oil cooking spray for greasing

Instructions:

1. **Preheat Oven and Prepare Pan**: Preheat your oven to 400°F (200°C). Lightly spray a baking sheet with canola oil cooking spray or line it with parchment paper.
2. **Prepare Veggies**: After grating the zucchinis and carrots, use a paper towel to squeeze out any excess moisture.
3. **Combine Ingredients**: In a large mixing bowl, combine the grated zucchini, grated carrot, beaten egg, oat flour, salt (if using), black pepper, dried thyme, and low-fat grated parmesan cheese. Mix well to form a homogenous batter.
4. **Shape Fritters**: Take small amounts of the mixture and form into flat, round fritter shapes. Place them onto the prepared baking sheet.
5. **Bake**: Place the baking sheet into the preheated oven. Bake for 20-25 minutes, flipping halfway through, until the fritters are golden brown on both sides.
6. **Serve**: Remove the fritters from the oven and let them cool slightly before serving. Enjoy them plain or with a gallbladder-friendly dipping sauce.

Nutritional Facts: Calories: 155 | Protein: 9g | Carbohydrates: 18g | Fiber: 4g | Sugars: 5g | Fat: 5g | Saturated Fat: 2g | Cholesterol: 90mg | Sodium: 330mg (if using salt)

Steamed Asparagus Spears with Lemon Zest

Preparation time: 10 minutes; Cooking time: 5 minutes; Serving size: 2 servings

Ingredients:

- 1 bunch of fresh asparagus spears (about 1/2 lb)
- Zest of 1 lemon
- 1/2 teaspoon salt (optional)
- Freshly ground black pepper to taste

Instructions:

1. **Prepare Asparagus**: Wash the asparagus thoroughly. Snap off the tough, woody ends from each spear.
2. **Prep the Lemon**: Wash the lemon well and grate its outer skin to get the zest.
3. **Steam Asparagus**: Fill a pot with about an inch of water and bring it to a boil. Place a steaming basket inside the pot, ensuring the water does not touch the bottom of the basket. Place the asparagus spears in the steaming basket, cover, and steam for 3 to 5 minutes, or until the asparagus is tender yet crisp.
4. **Season**: Remove the steamed asparagus from the basket and place it in a serving dish. Sprinkle the lemon zest over the top. If you're using salt, sprinkle it on as well, followed by a dash of freshly ground black pepper.
5. **Serve**: Serve immediately as a side dish or incorporate it into a main course.

Nutritional Facts: Calories: 20 | Protein: 2.2g | Carbohydrates: 3.9g | Fiber: 2g | Sugars: 1.9g | Fat: 0.2g | Saturated Fat: 0g | Cholesterol: 0mg | Sodium: 5mg

Baked Sweet Potato Fries with Paprika

Preparation time: 15 minutes; Cooking time: 30 minutes; Serving size: 2 servings

Ingredients:

- 2 medium-sized sweet potatoes
- 1/2 tablespoon olive oil
- 1 teaspoon paprika (adjust according to tolerance)
- 1/2 teaspoon salt (optional)
- 1/4 teaspoon black pepper (adjust according to tolerance)

Instructions:

1. **Preheat Oven**: Preheat your oven to 425°F (220°C). Line a baking sheet with parchment paper.
2. **Prepare Sweet Potatoes**: Wash and peel the sweet potatoes. Cut them into fries or wedges, making sure they are of uniform size for even cooking.
3. **Season**: In a large bowl, combine the sweet potato fries, olive oil, paprika, and black pepper. If using salt, add it as well. Toss well to ensure the fries are evenly coated with the seasoning.
4. **Arrange on Baking Sheet**: Place the seasoned sweet potato fries in a single layer on the lined baking sheet, making sure they are not crowded to ensure even cooking.
5. **Bake**: Place the baking sheet in the preheated oven and bake for 15 minutes. Then flip the fries and bake for another 10-15 minutes, or until they are crispy and golden brown.
6. **Serve**: Once done, remove from the oven and let cool for a couple of minutes before serving. Enjoy your Baked Sweet Potato Fries with Paprika as a snack or side dish!

Nutritional Facts: Calories: 180 | Protein: 2g | Carbohydrates: 40g | Fiber: 6g | Sugars: 13g | Fat: 3.5g | Saturated Fat: 0.3g | Cholesterol: 0mg | Sodium: 300mg (if using salt)

Garlic-Free Quinoa and Spinach Balls

Preparation time: 20 minutes; Cooking time: 25 minutes; Serving size: 2 servings

Ingredients:

- 1 cup cooked quinoa
- 1 cup fresh spinach, finely chopped
- 1 egg white, beaten
- 1/4 cup grated parmesan cheese (low-fat)
- 1/4 teaspoon salt (optional)
- 1/4 teaspoon black pepper (adjust according to tolerance)
- 1/2 teaspoon dried oregano
- 1 tablespoon olive oil for greasing

Instructions:

1. **Preheat Oven and Prepare Pan**: Preheat your oven to 375°F (190°C). Grease a baking sheet with olive oil or line it with parchment paper.
2. **Prepare Spinach**: Steam the spinach until wilted, approximately 3-4 minutes. Squeeze out excess water and chop finely.
3. **Mix Ingredients**: In a large bowl, combine the cooked quinoa, steamed spinach, beaten egg white, low-fat grated parmesan cheese, salt (if using), black pepper, and dried oregano. Mix well until all ingredients are well incorporated.
4. **Form Balls**: Using your hands, form the mixture into small balls, about 1-inch in diameter. Place them on the prepared baking sheet.
5. **Bake**: Put the baking sheet in the preheated oven and bake for about 20-25 minutes, or until the balls are golden brown and firm to the touch.
6. **Serve**: Once done, remove the quinoa and spinach balls from the oven and let them cool for a few minutes before serving. They can be served as is, or with a suitable dipping sauce that adheres to the post-surgical dietary guidelines.

Nutritional Facts: Calories: 210 | Protein: 12g | Carbohydrates: 27g | Fiber: 3g | Sugars: 1g | Fat: 6g | Saturated Fat: 2g | Cholesterol: 90mg | Sodium: 370mg (if using salt)

Smooth Chickpea and Beetroot Hummus

Preparation time: 10 minutes; Cooking time: 0 minutes; Serving size: 2 servings

Ingredients:

- 1 cup cooked chickpeas (canned or freshly cooked)
- 1 small beetroot, cooked and peeled
- 1 clove garlic, minced
- Juice of half a lemon
- 1 tablespoon tahini (optional)
- 1/2 teaspoon salt
- 1/4 teaspoon black pepper
- 2 tablespoons water
- Fresh herbs like parsley or chives for garnish (optional)

Instructions:

1. **Prepare Ingredients**: Ensure that the chickpeas are cooked and drained, and the beetroot is cooked, peeled, and chopped into smaller pieces.
2. **Blend Chickpeas and Beetroot**: In a food processor, add the chickpeas and beetroot. Blend until partially smooth.
3. **Add Seasonings and Liquid**: Add minced garlic, lemon juice, tahini (if using), salt, and black pepper to the food processor.
4. **Blend Again**: Blend the mixture until smooth. If it's too thick, add water one tablespoon at a time until you reach the desired consistency.
5. **Taste and Adjust**: Taste the hummus and adjust the seasoning if necessary.
6. **Garnish and Serve**: Transfer the hummus to a serving dish and garnish with fresh herbs like parsley or chives if you like.
7. **Storage**: Store any leftovers in an airtight container in the fridge for up to 5 days.

Nutritional Facts: Calories: 135 | Protein: 6g | Carbohydrates: 23g | Fiber: 6g | Sugars: 6g | Fat: 2g | Saturated Fat: 0g | Cholesterol: 0mg | Sodium: 600mg

Homemade Rice Crackers with Herbs

Preparation time: 15 minutes; Cooking time: 40 minutes; Serving size: 2 servings

Ingredients:

- 1 cup brown rice flour
- 1/2 teaspoon salt
- 1/4 teaspoon black pepper
- 1 teaspoon dried basil
- 1 teaspoon dried oregano
- 1/2 teaspoon garlic powder
- 1/4 cup water (more as needed)

Instructions:

1. **Preheat Oven**: Preheat your oven to 350°F (175°C). Line a baking sheet with parchment paper.
2. **Mix Dry Ingredients**: In a large bowl, combine brown rice flour, salt, black pepper, dried basil, dried oregano, and garlic powder. Mix well to combine.
3. **Add Water**: Slowly add water to the dry ingredients while stirring. You want the dough to come together but not be too wet. If the dough is crumbly, add a little more water until it holds together.
4. **Roll the Dough**: Place the dough between two sheets of parchment paper and roll it out as thinly as possible without breaking.
5. **Cut into Shapes**: Using a cookie cutter or a knife, cut the rolled dough into squares or circles. Carefully place them on the lined baking sheet.
6. **Bake**: Place the baking sheet in the preheated oven and bake for 20 minutes. Flip the crackers and continue baking for another 15-20 minutes or until they become crispy.
7. **Cool and Serve**: Remove from oven and allow the crackers to cool completely before serving. Store any leftovers in an airtight container for up to a week.

Nutritional Facts: Calories: 150 | Protein: 3g | Carbohydrates: 31g | Fiber: 2g | Sugars: 0g | Fat: 1g | Saturated Fat: 0g | Cholesterol: 0mg | Sodium: 290mg

Roasted Chickpeas with Sea Salt

Preparation time: 5 minutes; Cooking time: 25 minutes; Serving size: 2 servings

Ingredients:

- 1 can (about 15 oz or 425 g) chickpeas, drained and rinsed
- 1 teaspoon cooking spray (choose a gallbladder-friendly option)
- 1/4 teaspoon sea salt
- 1/4 teaspoon black pepper

Instructions:

1. **Preheat Oven**: Preheat your oven to 425°F (220°C).
2. **Prepare Chickpeas**: After draining and rinsing the chickpeas, pat them dry with a paper towel. Make sure they are thoroughly dry to ensure crispiness.
3. **Season Chickpeas**: Place the dried chickpeas in a bowl, and lightly spray with a cooking spray. Sprinkle with sea salt and black pepper, tossing to coat evenly.
4. **Arrange on Baking Sheet**: Line a baking sheet with parchment paper or a non-stick silicone mat. Spread the seasoned chickpeas in a single layer on the sheet.
5. **Roast**: Place the baking sheet in the preheated oven. Roast the chickpeas for 25 minutes, shaking the pan or stirring occasionally for even roasting.
6. **Check for Crispiness**: After 25 minutes, remove the chickpeas and test for crispiness. If they are not as crispy as you'd like, you can roast for an additional 5 minutes.
7. **Cool and Serve**: Allow the chickpeas to cool for a few minutes. They will continue to crisp as they cool. Serve immediately or store in an airtight container for later.

Nutritional Facts: Calories: 135 | Protein: 6g | Carbohydrates: 22g | Fiber: 6g | Sugars: 4g | Fat: 3g | Saturated Fat: 0.5g | Cholesterol: 0mg | Sodium: 325mg

Frozen Banana and Strawberry Bites

Preparation time: 10 minutes; Cooking time: 2 hours (freezing time); Serving size: 2 servings

Ingredients:

- 1 ripe banana, sliced into rounds
- 6 strawberries, halved
- 1 tablespoon honey or maple syrup (optional)

Instructions:

1. **Prepare the Fruit**: Peel the banana and slice it into rounds. Wash the strawberries and cut them in half.
2. **Arrange on Tray**: Place a sheet of parchment paper on a small tray or plate. Arrange the banana slices and strawberry halves on the parchment paper, ensuring they are not touching.
3. **Optional Sweetener**: If you're using honey or maple syrup, lightly drizzle it over the fruit slices.
4. **Freeze**: Place the tray in the freezer and let the fruit freeze for at least 2 hours, or until they are completely frozen.
5. **Assemble and Serve**: Once the fruits are frozen, quickly take them out of the freezer. Stack a banana slice and a strawberry half together, and serve immediately.
6. **Storage**: If not serving immediately, store the frozen bites in an airtight container in the freezer for up to a week.

Nutritional Facts: Calories: 95 | Protein: 1g | Carbohydrates: 24g | Fiber: 3g | Sugars: 14g | Fat: 0g | Saturated Fat: 0g | Cholesterol: 0mg | Sodium: 1mg

4.9 Desserts Recipes

Gluten-Free Apple Crumble with Oat Topping

Preparation time: 15 minutes; Cooking time: 30 minutes; Serving size: 2 servings

Ingredients:

For the apple Filling:

- 2 medium-sized apples, peeled, cored, and sliced (choose a variety like Fuji or Gala for natural sweetness)
- 1 tablespoon lemon juice
- 1 teaspoon cornstarch
- 1 tablespoon water
- 1 tablespoon honey or maple syrup (optional)

For the Oat Toping:

- 1/2 cup gluten-free rolled oats
- 2 tablespoons rice flour
- 1 tablespoon water
- 1 tablespoon sunflower oil (as a substitute for restricted oils)
- 1 teaspoon honey or maple syrup (optional)

Instructions:

1. **Preheat Oven**: Preheat your oven to 350°F (175°C). Grease a small baking dish with sunflower oil.
2. **Prepare the Apples**: Peel, core, and slice the apples. Toss them in a bowl with lemon juice.
3. **Cornstarch Slurry**: In a small bowl, mix cornstarch and water to make a slurry. Pour this into the bowl with the apples and mix well.
4. **Optional Sweetener**: If you wish to sweeten the apple filling, add honey or maple syrup. Mix well.
5. **Layer Apples**: Place the apple slices in the greased baking dish.
6. **Prepare the Topping**: In another bowl, mix the gluten-free oats, rice flour, water, and sunflower oil. Add honey or maple syrup if using.
7. **Add the Topping**: Sprinkle the oat mixture evenly over the apple slices.
8. **Bake**: Place the baking dish in the oven and bake for 30 minutes or until the top is golden brown and the apples are tender.
9. **Cool and Serve**: Let it cool for a few minutes before serving.

Nutritional Facts: Calories: 260 | Protein: 3g | Carbohydrates: 50g | Fiber: 6g | Sugars: 23g (without added sweeteners) | Fat: 6g | Saturated Fat: 1g | Cholesterol: 0mg | Sodium: 5mg

Oatmeal and Raisin Cookies (No Sugar Added)

Preparation time: 15 minutes; Cooking time: 12 minutes; Serving size: 2 servings (4 small cookies each)

Ingredients:

- 1 cup rolled oats
- 1/4 cup raisins
- 1 ripe banana, mashed
- 1/2 teaspoon vanilla extract
- 1/4 teaspoon baking soda
- 1/4 teaspoon salt
- 1/4 cup unsweetened applesauce
- 1 tablespoon sunflower oil

Instructions:

1. **Preheat Oven**: Preheat the oven to 350°F (175°C). Line a baking sheet with parchment paper.
2. **Mash the Banana**: In a medium bowl, mash the ripe banana until smooth.
3. **Combine Dry Ingredients**: In a separate bowl, mix together the rolled oats, baking soda, and salt.
4. **Mix Wet Ingredients**: Add the mashed banana, unsweetened applesauce, and vanilla extract to the dry ingredients.
5. **Add Oil**: Stir in 1 tablespoon of sunflower oil until the mixture is well combined.
6. **Add Raisins**: Fold in the raisins into the mixture.
7. **Shape Cookies**: Using a spoon, drop the batter onto the lined baking sheet to make small cookies. You should be able to make 8 small cookies.
8. **Bake**: Place the baking sheet in the preheated oven and bake for 12 minutes or until the cookies are slightly golden.
9. **Cool and Serve**: Allow the cookies to cool on the baking sheet for a few minutes before transferring them to a wire rack to cool completely.

Nutritional Facts: Calories: 180 | Protein: 3g | Carbohydrates: 34g | Fiber: 4g | Sugars: 12g (Natural sugars) | Fat: 4g | Saturated Fat: 0.3g | Cholesterol: 0mg | Sodium: 205mg

Almond Milk Rice Pudding with Vanilla Bean

Preparation time: 10 minutes; Cooking time: 40 minutes; Serving size: 2 servings

Ingredients:

- 1/2 cup short-grain brown rice
- 2 cups unsweetened almond milk
- 1/4 teaspoon salt
- 1 vanilla bean, split and seeds scraped
- 1 teaspoon ground cinnamon (optional)
- 1 tablespoon pure maple syrup
- 1 tablespoon cornstarch (optional, for thickening)
- Fresh fruit for garnish (e.g., blueberries or strawberries)

Instructions:

1. **Cook the Rice:** In a medium-sized pot, bring 2 cups of water to a boil. Add the brown rice and simmer on low heat until rice is tender, about 20 minutes. Drain excess water.
2. **Preheat Saucepan:** Place a medium-sized saucepan over low heat and add the cooked rice, unsweetened almond milk, salt, cinnamon and vanilla bean seeds along with the scraped pod.
3. **Stir and Simmer:** Stir the mixture well and allow it to simmer on low heat, stirring frequently to prevent sticking. Continue to simmer for approximately 20 minutes, until the mixture starts to thicken.
4. **Optional Thickening:** If you prefer a thicker consistency, mix 1 tablespoon of cornstarch with 2 tablespoons of almond milk and add it to the pot. Stir until fully combined.
5. **Add Maple Syrup:** Stir in the maple syrup, adjust for sweetness if desired.
6. **Remove Vanilla Bean:** Before serving, remember to remove the vanilla bean pod from the pot.
7. **Garnish and Serve:** Serve the rice pudding in bowls, garnished with fresh fruit.
8. **Optional:** If you like, you can use cinnamon for added flavor, but this is optional and should be omitted if you are avoiding cinnamon due to dietary restrictions.

Nutritional Facts: Calories: 250 | Protein: 5g | Carbohydrates: 45g | Fiber: 3g | Sugars: 11g | Fat: 5g | Saturated Fat: 0g | Cholesterol: 0mg | Sodium: 175mg

Zesty Orange and Pineapple Ice Pops

Preparation time: 15 minutes; Cooking time: 4 hours (freezing); Serving size: 2 servings

Ingredients:

- 1 cup fresh orange juice
- 1 cup fresh pineapple chunks
- 1 tablespoon agave nectar or maple syrup (optional)
- Zest of 1 orange
- 2 popsicle sticks

Instructions:

1. **Prepare the Fruit:** Zest one orange and set the zest aside. Juice the oranges until you have 1 cup of fresh juice. Cut the pineapple into small chunks.
2. **Blend:** In a blender, combine the fresh orange juice, pineapple chunks, and agave nectar or maple syrup, if using. Blend until smooth.
3. **Add Zest:** Stir in the orange zest into the blended mixture for an extra burst of flavor.
4. **Taste and Adjust:** Taste the mixture and adjust the sweetness with additional agave nectar or maple syrup, if desired.
5. **Pour into Molds:** Carefully pour the mixture into popsicle molds or small paper cups.
6. **Insert Sticks:** Place a popsicle stick into the center of each mold.
7. **Freeze:** Place the molds in the freezer and freeze for at least 4 hours, or until the ice pops are completely frozen.
8. **Unmold and Serve:** To unmold, run the popsicle molds under warm water for a few seconds, and then gently pull the sticks to remove the ice pops. Serve immediately.

Nutritional Facts: Calories: 90 | Protein: 1g | Carbohydrates: 21g | Fiber: 1g | Sugars: 17g | Fat: 0g | Saturated Fat: 0g | Cholesterol: 0mg | Sodium: 5mg

Homemade Banana and Blueberry Sorbet

Preparation time: 10 minutes; Cooking time: 0 minutes (Freezing time: 4 hours); Serving size: 2 servings

Ingredients:

- 2 ripe bananas, peeled and sliced
- 1 cup fresh blueberries
- 1 teaspoon lemon juice
- 2 tablespoons water
- 1 tablespoon honey or maple syrup (optional)

Instructions:

1. **Preparation**: Peel and slice the bananas into small pieces. Wash the blueberries and drain them well.
2. **Freeze**: Place the sliced bananas and blueberries in a ziplock bag or airtight container, and freeze for at least 4 hours or overnight.
3. **Blend**: Once the fruits are frozen, take them out of the freezer and place them into a blender. Add lemon juice and water to help in blending.
4. **Optional Sweetener**: If you want to add a touch of sweetness, add honey or maple syrup. Remember to use it sparingly, and only if you need it.
5. **Blend Again**: Blend until smooth. You might need to pause and scrape down the sides of the blender a few times to make sure everything is well-blended.
6. **Serve Immediately**: The sorbet is best served immediately for the most refreshing experience. If it's too soft, you can place it back in the freezer for another 20-30 minutes to firm up.
7. You can garnish with a few fresh blueberries or a small slice of banana before serving.

Nutritional Facts: Calories: 150 | Protein: 2g | Carbohydrates: 38g | Fiber: 5g | Sugars: 21g (without added sweeteners) | Fat: 0.5g | Saturated Fat: 0g | Cholesterol: 0mg | Sodium: 2mg

Vegan Chocolate Avocado Mousse

Preparation time: 15 minutes; Cooking time: 0 minutes; Serving size: 2 servings

Ingredients:

- 1 ripe avocado, peeled and pitted
- 1/4 cup unsweetened cocoa powder
- 1/4 cup unsweetened almond milk
- 2 tablespoons maple syrup (adjust to taste)
- 1 teaspoon vanilla extract
- A pinch of salt
- Fresh berries for garnish

Instructions:

1. **Prepare Avocado**: Cut the ripe avocado in half, remove the pit, and scoop the flesh into a blender or food processor.
2. **Add Ingredients to Blender**: Add the unsweetened cocoa powder, unsweetened almond milk, maple syrup, vanilla extract, and a pinch of salt to the blender.
3. **Blend Until Smooth**: Blend the mixture on high speed until it becomes completely smooth and creamy. You may need to pause and scrape down the sides of the blender to ensure everything is well-incorporated.
4. **Taste and Adjust**: Taste the mousse and adjust the sweetness by adding more maple syrup, if necessary.
5. **Chill**: Transfer the mousse to serving dishes and chill in the fridge for at least 1 hour to allow the flavors to meld and the texture to firm up slightly.
6. **Garnish and Serve**: Before serving, garnish with fresh berries.

Nutritional Facts: Calories: 200 | Protein: 3g | Carbohydrates: 25g | Fiber: 7g | Sugars: 12g | Fat: 12g | Saturated Fat: 2g | Cholesterol: 0mg | Sodium: 60mg

Peach and Raspberry Gelatin Cups

Preparation time: 10 minutes; Cooking time: 10 minutes; Serving size: 2 servings

Ingredients:

- 1 cup water
- 1 packet (7g) unflavored gelatin
- 1 tablespoon agave nectar or maple syrup
- 1 medium peach, diced
- 1/2 cup fresh raspberries
- Mint leaves for garnish (optional)

Instructions:

1. **Prepare Gelatin**: In a small saucepan, bring 1 cup of water to a boil. Once boiling, remove from heat and add the packet of unflavored gelatin. Stir until completely dissolved.
2. **Sweeten the Mixture**: Add 1 tablespoon of agave nectar or maple syrup to the gelatin mixture and stir well to combine.
3. **Prepare the Fruits**: Dice the peach and measure out the raspberries. Ensure that the fruits are thoroughly washed and dried.
4. **Assemble the Cups**: Evenly distribute the diced peaches and raspberries between two serving cups.
5. **Pour the Gelatin**: Slowly pour the gelatin mixture over the fruits in each cup, being careful to not disturb the arrangement of the fruits.
6. **Chill**: Place the cups in the refrigerator for at least 2-3 hours, or until the gelatin has fully set.
7. **Garnish and Serve**: Once the gelatin has set, you can garnish with mint leaves if desired, and enjoy your Peach and Raspberry Gelatin Cups.

Nutritional Facts: Calories: 60 | Protein: 2g | Carbohydrates: 14g | Fiber: 2g | Sugars: 10g | Fat: 0g | Saturated Fat: 0g | Cholesterol: 0mg | Sodium: 10mg

Baked Pears with a Drizzle of Maple Syrup

Preparation time: 10 minutes; Cooking time: 25 minutes; Serving size: 2 servings

Ingredients:

- 2 ripe pears, halved and cored
- 1 tablespoon lemon juice
- 1 tablespoons maple syrup
- Pinch of salt
- 1/4 cup water

Instructions:

1. **Preheat the Oven**: Preheat your oven to 350°F (175°C).
2. **Prepare the Pears**: Cut the pears in half and remove the core. Place them in a baking dish, cut side up.
3. **Add Lemon Juice**: Drizzle lemon juice over the pear halves.
4. **Season**: Sprinkle a pinch of salt over the pears.
5. **Add Water**: Pour 1/4 cup of water into the bottom of the baking dish to keep the pears moist as they bake.
6. **Bake**: Place the baking dish in the preheated oven and bake for 20-25 minutes or until the pears are soft.
7. **Maple Drizzle**: Once the pears are out of the oven, drizzle maple syrup evenly over the baked pears.
8. **Serve**: Serve the pears warm. They make a great dessert or a sweet side dish.

Nutritional Facts: Calories: 158 | Protein: 0.4g | Carbohydrates: 41g | Fiber: 5g | Sugars: 31g | Fat: 0.2g | Saturated Fat: 0g | Cholesterol: 0mg | Sodium: 58mg

Date and Nut Energy Balls (No Added Sugar)

Preparation time: 15 minutes; Cooking time: 0 minutes; Serving size: 2 servings

Ingredients:

- 6 Medjool dates, pitted
- 1/4 cup walnuts
- 1/4 cup cashews
- 1 tablespoon chia seeds
- 1 teaspoon vanilla extract

Instructions:

1. **Prepare the Ingredients**: Remove the pits from the Medjool dates and set aside. Measure out the walnuts, cashews, chia seeds, and vanilla extract.
2. **Blend the Nuts**: Place walnuts and cashews into a food processor and pulse until finely chopped.
3. **Add Dates and Seeds**: Add the pitted dates, chia seeds, and vanilla extract to the food processor.
4. **Process**: Blend all the ingredients together until a dough-like consistency is reached.
5. **Taste and Adjust**: You may taste the mixture at this point. If it's not sweet enough, you can add another date, but remember, the recipe aims to have no added sugar.
6. **Form Balls**: Take small amounts of the mixture and roll into balls using your hands.
7. **Chill**: Place the energy balls in the refrigerator for about 30 minutes to firm up before serving.
8. **Serve**: Enjoy your Date and Nut Energy Balls as a quick snack or as part of a balanced meal.

Nutritional Facts: Calories: 230 | Protein: 5g | Carbohydrates: 34g | Fiber: 5g | Sugars: 28g (natural sugars) | Fat: 10g | Saturated Fat: 1g | Cholesterol: 0mg | Sodium: 3mg

4.10 Smoothies and Beverages Recipes

Morning Bliss: Low-Fat Yogurt and Mixed Berry Smoothie

Preparation time: 5 minutes; Cooking time: 0 minutes; Serving size: 2 servings

Ingredients:

- 1 cup low-fat yogurt (plain, non-dairy alternatives can be used)
- 1 cup mixed berries (strawberries, blueberries, and raspberries), frozen or fresh
- 1 banana, sliced
- 1/2 cup unsweetened almond milk
- 1 tablespoon honey or maple syrup (optional)
- 1 teaspoon chia seeds (optional)

Instructions:

1. **Gather Ingredients**: Make sure you have all the ingredients in place—low-fat yogurt, mixed berries, banana, unsweetened almond milk, and optional sweeteners or chia seeds.
2. **Prepare the Blender**: Place your blender on the counter and plug it in. Ensure it is clean and ready to use.
3. **Blend Berries and Banana**: Add the mixed berries and sliced banana to the blender.
4. **Add Liquid**: Pour in the unsweetened almond milk and low-fat yogurt into the blender.
5. **Optional Add-ins**: If you're using honey or maple syrup for added sweetness or chia seeds for texture, add them now.
6. **Blend Until Smooth**: Close the lid of the blender and blend the mixture on high speed until you achieve a smooth consistency. This should take about 1-2 minutes.
7. **Taste and Adjust**: Give the smoothie a quick taste. If it's not sweet enough for your liking, you can add a bit more honey or maple syrup and blend again.
8. **Serve**: Pour the smoothie into glasses and enjoy your smoothie!

Nutritional Facts: Calories: 150 | Protein: 6g | Carbohydrates: 28g | Fiber: 4g | Sugars: 16g (natural sugars) | Fat: 2g | Saturated Fat: 0.5g | Cholesterol: 5mg | Sodium: 50mg

Tropical Paradise: Pineapple and Banana Smoothie

Preparation time: 5 minutes; Cooking time: 0 minutes; Serving size: 2 servings

Ingredients:

- 1 cup pineapple chunks, fresh or frozen
- 1 banana, sliced
- 1/2 cup low-fat yogurt (plain, non-dairy alternatives can be used)
- 1/2 cup unsweetened almond milk
- 1 tablespoon honey or maple syrup (optional)
- 1 teaspoon chia seeds (optional)

Instructions:

1. **Prepare the Ingredients**: Have all your ingredients ready—pineapple chunks, banana, low-fat yogurt, unsweetened almond milk, and optional sweeteners or chia seeds.
2. **Set Up Blender**: Position your blender on the counter and make sure it's clean and plugged in.
3. **Blend Pineapple and Banana**: Add the pineapple chunks and sliced banana to the blender.
4. **Pour in Liquids**: Add the unsweetened almond milk and low-fat yogurt to the blender.
5. **Optional Add-Ins**: If you wish to include honey or maple syrup for additional sweetness, or chia seeds for texture, add them now.
6. **Blend Until Smooth**: Secure the blender's lid and blend on high speed until the mixture is smooth. This should take around 1-2 minutes.
7. **Taste Test**: Sample the smoothie. If you find it needs more sweetness, add a little more honey or maple syrup and blend again.
8. **Pour and Enjoy**: Once the smoothie has reached your desired taste and consistency, pour it into glasses and enjoy your smoothie immediately!

Nutritional Facts: Calories: 145 | Protein: 5g | Carbohydrates: 30g | Fiber: 3g | Sugars: 18g (natural sugars) | Fat: 1g | Saturated Fat: 0.3g | Cholesterol: 3mg | Sodium: 40mg

Peachy Keen: Peach and Almond Milk Smoothie

Preparation time: 5 minutes; Cooking time: 0 minutes; Serving size: 2 servings

Ingredients:

- 2 medium-sized peaches, pitted and sliced
- 1 cup unsweetened almond milk
- 1/2 teaspoon vanilla extract
- 1 tablespoon honey or maple syrup (optional)
- Ice cubes (optional)

Instructions:

1. **Prepare the Peaches**: Wash, pit, and slice the peaches.
2. **Get the Blender Ready**: Place your blender on a stable surface and make sure it's plugged in.
3. **Blend the Peaches**: Add the sliced peaches to the blender.
4. **Add Almond Milk**: Pour in the unsweetened almond milk.
5. **Flavor with Vanilla**: Add a half teaspoon of vanilla extract to the blender for flavor.
6. **Optional Sweetness**: If you prefer your smoothies on the sweeter side, add a tablespoon of honey or maple syrup.
7. **Optional Ice**: If you like your smoothies cold, add some ice cubes to the blender.
8. **Blend Until Smooth**: Secure the lid and blend on high speed until you get a smooth texture, usually about 1-2 minutes.
9. **Taste and Adjust**: Give your smoothie a taste. If you think it needs more sweetness, add a bit more honey or maple syrup and blend again.
10. **Serve and Enjoy**: Once the smoothie is to your liking, pour into glasses and enjoy immediately.

Nutritional Facts: Calories: 118 | Protein: 2g | Carbohydrates: 24g | Fiber: 3g | Sugars: 20g (natural sugars) | Fat: 2g | Saturated Fat: 0g | Cholesterol: 0mg | Sodium: 85mg

Berry Bonanza: Strawberry and Raspberry Smoothie

Preparation time: 10 minutes; Cooking time: 0 minutes; Serving size: 2 servings

Ingredients:

- 1 cup fresh strawberries, washed and hulled
- 1 cup fresh raspberries, washed
- 1 cup low-fat almond milk or skim milk
- 1 banana, peeled and sliced
- 1 tablespoon chia seeds (optional)
- 1-2 teaspoons stevia or monk fruit sweetener (optional)
- Ice cubes (optional)

Instructions:

1. **Prepare the Fruit**: Wash the strawberries and raspberries thoroughly and remove any stems or leaves.
2. **Slice the Banana**: Peel the banana and slice it into small pieces.
3. **Blend**: In a blender, add the strawberries, raspberries, and sliced banana.
4. **Add Liquid**: Pour in the low-fat almond milk or skim milk to help with blending.
5. **Optional Add-ins**: If you are using chia seeds and/or a sweetener, add them to the blender.
6. **Blend Again**: Secure the lid on the blender and blend until the mixture is smooth. If the mixture is too thick, you can add a little more almond milk to reach your desired consistency.
7. **Ice Option**: If you like your smoothies cold, add some ice cubes to the blender and blend until smooth.
8. **Serve**: Once the smoothie has reached your preferred consistency, pour it into two glasses and serve immediately.

Nutritional Facts: Calories: 110 | Protein: 2g | Carbohydrates: 25g | Fiber: 7g | Sugars: 14g | Fat: 1.5g | Saturated Fat: 0g | Cholesterol: 0mg | Sodium: 95mg

Apple Orchard: Apple Juice with a Splash of Lime

Preparation time: 5 minutes; Cooking time: 0 minutes; Serving size: 2 servings

Ingredients:

- 2 cups fresh apple juice (preferably cold-pressed and without added sugar)
- Juice of half a lime
- A pinch of sea salt (optional)
- Ice cubes (optional)
- Fresh mint leaves for garnish (optional)

Instructions:

1. **Prepare Apple Juice**: If you are making fresh apple juice, juice your apples until you have 2 cups. If using store-bought, make sure it is cold-pressed and has no added sugar.
2. **Lime Juice**: Cut a lime in half and juice one half. Save the other half for another use or for garnishing.
3. **Mix**: In a jug, combine the fresh apple juice and lime juice. Stir well to mix the flavors.
4. **Optional Add-ins**: If you want to enhance the flavor, you can add a pinch of sea salt.
5. **Ice Option**: If you prefer your drinks cold, add some ice cubes to the jug or directly into the serving glasses.
6. **Garnish and Serve**: If using, garnish with a fresh mint leaf. Pour into two glasses and serve immediately.

Nutritional Facts: Calories: 95 | Protein: 0.2g | Carbohydrates: 24g | Fiber: 0.2g | Sugars: 22g | Fat: 0.3g | Saturated Fat: 0g | Cholesterol: 0mg | Sodium: 10mg

Refresh-Mint: Lemon and Mint Iced Herbal Tea

Preparation time: 5 minutes; Cooking time: 10 minutes; Serving size: 2 servings

Ingredients:

- 2 cups water
- 1 lemon, thinly sliced
- A handful of fresh mint leaves
- 1 tablespoon honey or maple syrup (optional)
- Ice cubes

Instructions:

1. **Boil Water**: In a saucepan, bring 2 cups of water to a boil.
2. **Add Mint**: Once the water reaches a rolling boil, add the fresh mint leaves.
3. **Simmer**: Reduce heat to low and let the mint leaves simmer in the water for 5 minutes.
4. **Strain**: After simmering, remove the saucepan from heat. Use a strainer to remove the mint leaves, collecting the infused water in a jug or bowl.
5. **Add Lemon**: Place the thinly sliced lemon into the mint-infused water while it is still hot.
6. **Sweeten**: Add a tablespoon of honey or maple syrup while the water is still warm. Stir until fully dissolved.
7. **Cool**: Allow the lemon and mint-infused water to cool to room temperature or place it in the fridge to chill faster.
8. **Serve Over Ice**: Once chilled, serve the lemon and mint herbal tea over ice cubes in glasses.
9. **Garnish and Serve**: Optionally, garnish with a mint leaf or a lemon slice before serving.

Nutritional Facts: Calories: 20 | Protein: 0g | Carbohydrates: 6g | Fiber: 0g | Sugars: 5g (if sweetened) | Fat: 0g | Saturated Fat: 0g | Cholesterol: 0mg | Sodium: 10mg

Carrot Bliss: Carrot and Orange Juice Blend

Preparation time: 10 minutes; Cooking time: 0 minutes; Serving size: 2 servings

Ingredients:

- 4 medium-sized carrots, peeled and cut into chunks
- 2 large oranges, peeled and segmented
- 1 small piece of fresh ginger, about 1-inch, peeled (optional)
- 1 cup of cold water
- Ice cubes for serving (optional)

Instructions:

1. **Prepare Ingredients**: Peel the carrots and cut them into manageable chunks. Peel the oranges and separate them into segments. If you are using ginger, peel and cut it into a small piece.
2. **Juice the Carrots and Oranges**: Using a juicer, juice the carrots, oranges, and ginger (if using).
3. **Combine and Mix**: In a blender, combine the carrot juice, orange juice, and optional ginger juice. Add 1 cup of cold water and blend until smooth. If you don't have a juicer, you can also blend the carrots, oranges, and ginger with water and then strain the mixture to get the juice.
4. **Taste and Adjust**: Sample the juice and adjust the water ratio if necessary.
5. **Serve**: Divide the juice evenly into two glasses. Add ice cubes if you prefer a colder drink.

Nutritional Facts: Calories: 95 | Protein: 2g | Carbohydrates: 23g | Fiber: 4g | Sugars: 17g | Fat: 0g | Saturated Fat: 0g | Cholesterol: 0mg | Sodium: 75mg

Mango Tango: Mango and Coconut Water Smoothie

Preparation time: 10 minutes; Cooking time: 0 minutes; Serving size: 2 servings

Ingredients:

- 1 large ripe mango, peeled and pitted
- 1.5 cups coconut water (unsweetened)
- 1 tablespoon chia seeds (optional)
- A pinch of sea salt (optional)
- Ice cubes (optional)
- Fresh mint or basil leaves for garnish (optional)

Instructions:

1. **Prepare Mango**: Peel and pit the mango. Cut it into smaller chunks for easier blending.
2. **Blend**: Add the mango chunks and coconut water to a blender. Blend on high speed until smooth.
3. **Optional Add-ins**: If you are using chia seeds for extra fiber and nutrients, add them to the blender and pulse a couple of times to mix. If using, add a pinch of sea salt to enhance the flavors.
4. **Ice Option**: If you prefer your smoothies cold, you can add a handful of ice cubes to the blender and pulse again until the ice is crushed and the smoothie is chilled.
5. **Garnish and Serve**: Pour the smoothie into two glasses. If using, garnish with a sprig of fresh mint or basil.

Nutritional Facts: Calories: 120 | Protein: 2g | Carbohydrates: 28g | Fiber: 3g | Sugars: 25g | Fat: 1g | Saturated Fat: 0g | Cholesterol: 0mg | Sodium: 115mg

Soothing Ginger: Warm Ginger and Lemon Herbal Tea

Preparation time: 5 minutes; Cooking time: 10 minutes; Serving size: 2 servings

Ingredients:

- 1-inch fresh ginger root, peeled and thinly sliced
- 1 lemon, sliced into rounds
- 4 cups of water
- 1-2 teaspoons of honey or maple syrup (optional)

Instructions:

1. **Preparation**: Peel the ginger root and slice it thinly. Slice the lemon into rounds.
2. **Boil Water**: In a saucepan, bring 4 cups of water to a gentle boil.
3. **Add Ginger**: Once the water is boiling, add the sliced ginger to the saucepan.
4. **Simmer**: Reduce heat and let the ginger simmer for about 7-8 minutes.
5. **Add Lemon**: Add the sliced lemon to the saucepan and let it simmer for an additional 2 minutes.
6. **Strain and Serve**: Turn off the heat and strain the herbal tea into teacups.
7. **Sweeten If Desired**: If you wish, you can add 1-2 teaspoons of honey or maple syrup to sweeten the tea. Stir well before drinking.
8. **Enjoy**: Sip your warm ginger and lemon herbal tea. It's not only soothing but also aids in digestion.

Nutritional Facts: Calories: 20 | Protein: 0.5g | Carbohydrates: 6g | Fiber: 0.2g | Sugars: 4g (if honey is added) | Fat: 0g | Saturated Fat: 0g | Cholesterol: 0mg | Sodium: 10mg

Chapter 5: Special Occasion Recipes

When special days roll around, the joy of celebrating with loved ones is often centered around a shared table of delightful dishes. This chapter is your essential guide to crafting memorable meals, tailored especially for those who've had gallbladder challenges. Whether you're looking to prepare festive and holiday dishes that capture the essence of the season, or you're hosting friends and want to serve dishes that leave a lasting impression, this chapter ensures that your culinary creations resonate with care, flavor, and thoughtfulness.

5.1 Festive and holiday dishes

New Year's Eve Lobster Tail with Grapefruit and Basil Salsa

Preparation time: 20 minutes; Cooking time: 12 minutes; Serving size: 2 servings

Ingredients:

- 2 lobster tails (about 5 oz or 140 g, each)
- 1 tablespoon corn oil
- Salt to taste
- 1 lemon, cut into wedges, for serving
- 1 grapefruit, peeled and segmented
- 1/4 cup finely chopped fresh basil
- 1 small shallot, finely chopped
- Salt to taste

Instructions:

1. **Preheat the Grill:**
   - Preheat your grill to high heat, or if using an oven, preheat the broiler.
2. **Prepare the Lobster Tail:**
   - Using kitchen scissors, cut the top shell of the lobster tails lengthwise but leave the tail fan intact.
   - Pull apart the shells slightly and brush the lobster meat with corn oil.
   - Sprinkle with a pinch of salt.
3. **Cook the Lobster Tail:**
   - Place the lobster tails shell-side down on the preheated grill.
   - Grill for 5-7 minutes, or until the lobster meat is opaque.
   - Alternatively, you can broil the lobster tails for 5-7 minutes in the oven.
4. **Make the Grapefruit and Basil Salsa:**
   - In a small mixing bowl, combine grapefruit segments, chopped basil, and finely chopped shallot.
   - Add a pinch of salt and mix well.
5. **Assemble and Serve:**
   - Place the grilled or broiled lobster tails on a serving platter.
   - Spoon the grapefruit and basil salsa over the lobster.
   - Serve with lemon wedges on the side.

Nutritional Facts: Calories: 290 | Protein: 28g | Carbohydrates: 15g | Fiber: 2g | Sugars: 9g | Fat: 12g | Saturated Fat: 1g | Cholesterol: 90mg | Sodium: 480mg | Potassium: 370mg

Caramelized Onion and Saffron Risotto with Roasted Bell Peppers

Preparation time: 20 minutes; Cooking time: 40 minutes; Serving size: 2 servings

Ingredients:

For the Risotto:

- 1 cup Arborio rice (brown rice can be substituted for a healthier option)
- 1 medium onion, thinly sliced
- 1 teaspoon saffron threads
- 4 cups low-sodium vegetable broth
- 1 tablespoon canola oil
- Salt to taste

For the Roasted Bell Peppers:

- 2 bell peppers, sliced
- 1 teaspoon canola oil
- Salt to taste

Instructions:

1. **Preheat the Oven for Bell Peppers**:
   - Preheat the oven to 400°F (200°C).
2. **Prepare the Bell Peppers**:
   - Toss the sliced bell peppers in canola oil and salt.
   - Lay them on a baking sheet in a single layer.
   - Roast in the oven for about 15-20 minutes until tender but still crisp.
3. **Prepare the Broth**:
   - In a small pot, warm the vegetable broth over low heat.
   - Add the saffron threads to the broth to steep.
4. **Caramelize the Onions**:
   - In a large pan, heat 1 tablespoon of canola oil over medium heat.
   - Add the thinly sliced onion and cook, stirring occasionally until they are caramelized, about 15 minutes.
5. **Cook the Risotto**:
   - Add the Arborio rice to the pan with the onions and stir well to coat the rice.
   - Begin adding the saffron-infused vegetable broth one cup at a time, stirring continuously.
   - Wait until the liquid is mostly absorbed before adding the next cup.
   - Continue this process until the rice is al dente and creamy, about 18-20 minutes.
6. **Combine and Serve**:
   - Divide the risotto into two bowls.
   - Top with roasted bell peppers.
   - Optional: Garnish with fresh parsley for added flavor and aesthetic.

Nutritional Facts: Calories: 420 | Protein: 9g | Carbohydrates: 75g | Fiber: 5g | Sugars: 6g | Fat: 9g | Saturated Fat: 1g | Cholesterol: 0mg | Sodium: 400mg | Potassium: 420mg

Exotic Thai-Inspired Mango and Papaya Salad with Chilled Shrimp

Preparation time: 25 minutes; Cooking time: 5 minutes; Serving size: 2 servings

Ingredients:

For the Salad:

- 1 medium ripe mango, peeled and diced
- 1 medium ripe papaya, peeled and diced
- 12 large shrimp, peeled and deveined
- 1 cup of mixed greens (lettuce, spinach)
- 1/4 cup fresh cilantro leaves
- 1/4 cup fresh mint leaves

For the Dressing:

- 2 tablespoons rice vinegar
- 1 teaspoon grape seed oil
- 1 teaspoon honey
- Salt to taste

Instructions:

1. **Cook the Shrimp:**
   - Bring a pot of water to a boil.
   - Add the shrimp and cook for about 2-3 minutes or until they turn pink and opaque.
   - Remove shrimp from water and immediately place them in a bowl of ice water to chill.
2. **Prepare the Fruits:**
   - Dice the mango and papaya into bite-sized pieces and set them aside.
3. **Make the Dressing:**
   - In a small bowl, whisk together the rice vinegar, grape seed oil, honey, and salt until well combined.
4. **Assemble the Salad:**
   - In a large mixing bowl, combine the mixed greens, mango, papaya, cilantro, and mint leaves.
   - Add the chilled shrimp on top.
5. **Dress and Serve:**
   - Drizzle the dressing over the salad and gently toss to combine.
   - Divide the salad between two plates and serve immediately.

Nutritional Facts: Calories: 270 | Protein: 15g | Carbohydrates: 35g | Fiber: 5g | Sugars: 25g | Fat: 8g | Saturated Fat: 1g | Cholesterol: 90mg | Sodium: 250mg | Potassium: 450mg

Champagne-Poached Pear Salad with Arugula and Toasted Walnuts

Preparation time: 20 minutes; Cooking time: 30 minutes; Serving size: 2 servings

Ingredients:

For the Poached Pears:

- 2 ripe but firm pears, peeled, cored, and halved
- 1 bottle of non-alcoholic champagne or sparkling water
- 1 teaspoon of lemon juice

For the Salad:

- 4 cups of fresh arugula, washed and dried
- 1/4 cup of walnuts, toasted
- 1 teaspoon sunflower oil
- Salt to taste

Instructions:

1. **Poach the Pears**:
   - In a saucepan, bring the non-alcoholic champagne and lemon juice to a simmer.
   - Add the pear halves and simmer for about 20-25 minutes, or until the pears are tender but not mushy.
   - Remove the pears from the liquid and allow them to cool to room temperature.
2. **Toast the Walnuts**:
   - In a dry skillet over medium heat, toast the walnuts for about 3-5 minutes, stirring frequently, until they become fragrant. Remove from heat and let cool.
3. **Prepare the Arugula**:
   - In a large mixing bowl, toss the arugula with sunflower oil and a pinch of salt.
4. **Assemble the Salad**:
   - Slice the poached pears into thin wedges.
   - Divide the arugula between two plates and top with the pear slices.
   - Sprinkle the toasted walnuts over the top of each salad.
5. **Serve**:
   - Serve immediately, optionally drizzling a little more sunflower oil over the top if desired.

Nutritional Facts: Calories: 270 | Protein: 3g | Carbohydrates: 40g | Fiber: 6g | Sugars: 26g | Fat: 12g | Saturated Fat: 1g | Cholesterol: 0mg | Sodium: 20mg | Potassium: 350mg

Winter Harvest Vegetable Wellington with Quinoa Filling

Preparation time: 30 minutes; Cooking time: 45 minutes; Serving size: 2 servings

Ingredients:

For the Quinoa Filling:

- 1/2 cup quinoa, rinsed
- 1 cup vegetable broth (low sodium)

For the Vegetable Layer:

- 1 medium carrot, thinly sliced
- 1 zucchini, thinly sliced
- 1/2 red bell pepper, thinly sliced
- 1/2 yellow bell pepper, thinly sliced

For the Assembly:

- 1 sheet whole-grain puff pastry (thawed, if frozen)
- 1 tablespoon unsweetened almond milk
- Salt and pepper to taste

Instructions:

1. **Cook Quinoa**: In a small pot, combine quinoa and vegetable broth. Bring to a boil, then reduce heat to low, cover, and simmer for 15 minutes or until the quinoa is tender and liquid is absorbed.
2. **Preheat Oven**: Preheat your oven to 375°F (190°C).
3. **Prepare Vegetables**: Slice the carrot, zucchini, and bell peppers thinly. Lightly steam them until they are just tender but not mushy.
4. **Assembly**:
   - Lay the puff pastry sheet on a parchment-lined baking tray.
   - Place the cooked quinoa in the center of the puff pastry sheet, spreading it out but leaving ample space at the edges.
   - Layer the steamed vegetables on top of the quinoa.
5. **Season and Fold**: Sprinkle a little salt and pepper on the vegetable layer. Fold the puff pastry over the quinoa and vegetable layers, sealing the edges.
6. **Brush and Bake**:
   - Lightly brush the top of the Wellington with unsweetened almond milk.
   - Place the tray in the preheated oven and bake for 30 minutes or until the puff pastry is golden brown.
7. **Cool and Serve**: Remove from oven and allow it to cool for a few minutes before slicing and serving.

Nutritional Facts: Calories: 410 | Protein: 12g | Carbohydrates: 55g | Fiber: 8g | Sugars: 6g | Fat: 16g | Saturated Fat: 1.5g | Cholesterol: 0mg | Sodium: 250mg | Potassium: 650mg

Easter Poached Sea Bass with Lemon-Fennel Broth

Preparation time: 15 minutes; Cooking time: 20 minutes; Serving size: 2 servings

Ingredients:

For the Sea Bass:

- 2 sea bass fillets (about 6 oz or 170 g, each)
- Salt and pepper to taste
- 4 cups water for poaching

For the Lemon-Fennel Broth:

- 1 small fennel bulb, thinly sliced
- Zest and juice of 1 lemon
- 2 cups low-sodium chicken or vegetable broth
- 1 teaspoon sunflower oil

Instructions:

1. **Prepare the Broth**:
   - In a saucepan, heat sunflower oil over medium heat.
   - Add thinly sliced fennel and sauté until softened, about 5 minutes.
   - Add the low-sodium broth, lemon zest, and juice to the saucepan.
   - Bring to a simmer and cook for about 10 minutes, allowing flavors to meld.
   - Strain the broth to remove fennel and set aside, keeping warm.
2. **Poach the Sea Bass**:
   - Fill a separate, deep pan with 4 cups of water and bring to a gentle simmer.
   - Season sea bass fillets with salt and pepper.
   - Carefully lower the fillets into the simmering water.
   - Poach for 6-8 minutes, or until the fish flakes easily with a fork.
3. **Combine and Serve**:
   - Place each poached sea bass fillet in a deep serving bowl.
   - Pour the warm Lemon-Fennel Broth over the fish.
   - Optional: Garnish with fresh fennel fronds for added flavor and aesthetic.

Nutritional Facts: Calories: 180 | Protein: 30g | Carbohydrates: 8g | Fiber: 2g | Sugars: 4g | Fat: 4g | Saturated Fat: 1g | Cholesterol: 70mg | Sodium: 350mg | Potassium: 620mg

Valentine's Day Grilled Oysters with Cucumber and Dill Mignonette

Preparation time: 15 minutes; Cooking time: 5 minutes; Serving size: 2 servings

Ingredients:

- 12 fresh oysters, cleaned and shucked
- 1 tablespoon corn oil for grilling
- 1/4 cup rice vinegar
- 1/4 cup finely chopped cucumber
- 1 tablespoon chopped fresh dill
- Salt and pepper to taste

Instructions:

1. **Preheat Grill**:
   - Preheat your grill to high heat.
2. **Prepare the Mignonette**:
   - In a small mixing bowl, combine the rice vinegar, finely chopped cucumber, fresh dill, salt, and pepper.
   - Mix well and set aside to let the flavors meld.
3. **Prepare Oysters for Grilling**:
   - Lightly brush the oysters with corn oil to prevent them from sticking to the grill.
4. **Grill the Oysters**:
   - Place the oysters on the preheated grill.
   - Cover and grill for 4-5 minutes, or until the oysters just begin to open.
5. **Serve**:
   - Once the oysters are done, remove them from the grill carefully.
   - Arrange them on a serving platter and spoon a little of the Cucumber and Dill Mignonette over each oyster.
   - Serve immediately.

Nutritional Facts: Calories: 85 | Protein: 6g | Carbohydrates: 4g | Fiber: 0g | Sugars: 1g | Fat: 5g | Saturated Fat: 1g | Cholesterol: 25mg | Sodium: 120mg | Potassium: 100mg

Fig and Walnut-Stuffed Butternut Squash Roast

Preparation time: 20 minutes; Cooking time: 50 minutes; Serving size: 2 servings

Ingredients:

For the Butternut Squash:

- 1 medium butternut squash, halved lengthwise and seeds removed
- 1 tablespoon olive oil

For the Filling:

- 1/2 cup chopped dried figs
- 1/2 cup chopped walnuts
- 1/2 cup cooked quinoa
- 1 tablespoon maple syrup
- 1/2 teaspoon fresh thyme leaves
- Salt to taste

For the Glaze:

- 2 tablespoons apple cider vinegar
- 1 tablespoon maple syrup

Instructions:

1. **Preheat Oven:**
   - Preheat your oven to 400°F (200°C).
2. **Prepare the Butternut Squash:**
   - Rub the halved butternut squash with olive oil and place it on a baking sheet, cut-side down.
   - Roast for 30 minutes or until tender but still firm.
3. **Prepare the Filling:**
   - In a medium mixing bowl, combine the chopped dried figs, walnuts, cooked quinoa, maple syrup, fresh thyme leaves, and salt.
4. **Stuff the Squash:**
   - After the squash is done roasting, carefully flip them over.
   - Spoon the fig and walnut mixture into the hollowed parts of the squash.
5. **Make the Glaze:**
   - In a small bowl, mix the apple cider vinegar and maple syrup.
6. **Glaze and Roast Again:**
   - Drizzle the glaze over the stuffed squash.
   - Return to the oven and roast for another 15-20 minutes, or until the filling is warm and slightly crispy.
7. **Serve:**
   - Once done, remove from the oven and allow it to cool for a few minutes before serving.

Nutritional Facts: Calories: 380 | Protein: 6g | Carbohydrates: 52g | Fiber: 9g | Sugars: 30g | Fat: 18g | Saturated Fat: 2g | Cholesterol: 0mg | Sodium: 20mg | Potassium: 700mg

5.2 Meals for entertaining guests

Stuffed Mini Bell Peppers with Quinoa and Grilled Vegetables

Preparation time: 20 minutes; Cooking time: 30 minutes; Serving size: 2 servings

Ingredients:

For the Quinoa:
- 1/2 cup quinoa
- 1 cup water

For the Grilled Vegetables:
- 1 small zucchini, sliced
- 1 small yellow squash, sliced
- 1/2 red onion, sliced

For the Stuffed Peppers:
- 6 mini bell peppers, halved and seeds removed
- Fresh parsley for garnish

For the Dressing:
- 2 tablespoons lemon juice
- 1 teaspoon Dijon mustard
- Salt and pepper to taste

Instructions:

1. **Cook the Quinoa:**
   - Rinse quinoa under cold water.
   - In a saucepan, bring 1 cup of water to a boil. Add quinoa, reduce heat to low, cover, and simmer for 15 minutes or until quinoa is cooked. Fluff with a fork and set aside.
2. **Grill the Vegetables:**
   - Preheat the grill to medium heat.
   - Grill the zucchini, yellow squash, and red onion slices for about 5 minutes on each side or until they have nice grill marks. Remove and set aside.
3. **Prepare the Dressing:**
   - In a small bowl, whisk together lemon juice, Dijon mustard, salt, and pepper.
4. **Combine Quinoa and Vegetables:**
   - In a large bowl, mix the cooked quinoa with the grilled vegetables. Add the dressing and toss to combine.
5. **Stuff the Peppers:**
   - Preheat the oven to 350°F (175°C).
   - Spoon the quinoa and vegetable mixture into the halved mini bell peppers.
6. **Bake:**
   - Place the stuffed peppers on a baking sheet lined with parchment paper.
   - Bake for 15-20 minutes, or until the peppers are tender.
7. **Garnish and Serve:**
   - Garnish with fresh parsley before serving.

Nutritional Facts: Calories: 230 | Protein: 9g | Carbohydrates: 40g | Fiber: 7g | Sugars: 9g | Fat: 5g | Saturated Fat: 0.5g | Cholesterol: 0mg | Sodium: 80mg | Potassium: 780mg

Veggie Sushi Rolls with Brown Rice

Preparation time: 40 minutes; Cooking time: 45 minutes; Serving size: 2 servings

Ingredients:

For the Brown Rice:
- 1 cup brown rice
- 2 cups water

For the Sushi Vinegar:
- 2 tablespoons rice vinegar
- 1 tablespoon sugar (or sugar substitute)
- 1/2 teaspoon salt

For the Veggie Filling:
- 1/2 cucumber, julienned
- 1/2 avocado, sliced thinly
- 1/2 red bell pepper, julienned
- 1/2 carrot, julienned

Other:
- 2 sheets nori seaweed
- Optional: low-sodium soy sauce for dipping

Instructions:

1. **Cook the Brown Rice:**
   - Rinse the brown rice under cold water.
   - In a saucepan, bring 2 cups of water to a boil. Add the brown rice and reduce heat to low. Cover and simmer for 45 minutes, or until rice is cooked. Remove from heat and let it cool.
2. **Prepare Sushi Vinegar:**
   - In a small saucepan, combine rice vinegar, sugar, and salt. Heat on low until the sugar dissolves. Let it cool.
3. **Mix Rice and Vinegar:**
   - Transfer the cooked brown rice to a large bowl and add the sushi vinegar. Mix thoroughly to combine. Allow rice to cool to room temperature.
4. **Prepare Veggies:**
   - Julienne the cucumber, red bell pepper, and carrot. Thinly slice the avocado.
5. **Assemble Sushi Rolls:**
   - Place a sheet of plastic wrap on a sushi rolling mat.
   - Lay one sheet of nori on the plastic wrap.
   - Wet your fingers to prevent sticking and spread an even layer of brown rice onto the nori, leaving a small margin at the top and bottom.
   - Lay out the veggies horizontally across the middle of the rice.
6. **Roll and Slice:**
   - Using the sushi mat, roll the sushi tightly.
   - With a sharp knife, cut the roll into 1-inch pieces.
7. **Serve:**
   - Serve the Veggie Sushi Rolls with low-sodium soy sauce, if desired.

Nutritional Facts: Calories: 320 | Protein: 7g | Carbohydrates: 65g | Fiber: 6g | Sugars: 6g | Fat: 5g | Saturated Fat: 1g | Cholesterol: 0mg | Sodium: 300mg | Potassium: 400mg

Sweet Potato and Black Bean Pinwheels

Preparation time: 20 minutes; Cooking time: 30 minutes; Serving size: 2 servings
Ingredients:

For the Sweet Potato Mash:

- 1 medium sweet potato, peeled and diced
- 1 teaspoon grapeseed oil
- Salt and pepper to taste

For the Black Bean Mixture:

- 1/2 cup canned black beans, drained and rinsed
- 1 teaspoon cumin
- Salt and pepper to taste

For the Pinwheels:

- 2 whole-grain tortillas
- 1/2 cup baby spinach, finely chopped

Instructions:

1. **Prepare the Sweet Potato Mash:**
   - Preheat the oven to 400°F (200°C).
   - Toss the sweet potato cubes with grapeseed oil, salt, and pepper.
   - Spread them on a baking sheet and roast for 20 minutes or until tender.
   - Once cooked, mash the sweet potatoes in a bowl and set aside.
2. **Prepare the Black Bean Mixture:**
   - In a bowl, mash the black beans.
   - Add cumin, salt, and pepper. Mix until well combined.
3. **Assemble the Pinwheels:**
   - Lay out the whole-grain tortillas on a flat surface.
   - Spread an even layer of sweet potato mash on each tortilla.
   - Add a layer of the black bean mixture.
   - Sprinkle chopped baby spinach over the black bean layer.
4. **Roll and Slice:**
   - Carefully roll up each tortilla, keeping it as tight as possible.
   - Using a sharp knife, cut each roll into 1-inch pinwheels.
5. **Serve:**
   - Arrange the pinwheels on a plate, and they are ready to be served.

Nutritional Facts: Calories: 285 | Protein: 8g | Carbohydrates: 50g | Fiber: 10g | Sugars: 6g | Fat: 6g | Saturated Fat: 1g | Cholesterol: 0mg | Sodium: 200mg | Potassium: 500mg

Grilled Zucchini and Tomato Skewers

Preparation time: 20 minutes; Cooking time: 10 minutes; Serving size: 2 servings

Ingredients:

- 2 medium zucchinis, cut into 1-inch rounds
- 1 cup cherry tomatoes
- 1 tablespoon canola oil
- Salt and pepper to taste
- Fresh basil leaves for garnish

Instructions:

1. **Preheat the Grill:**
   - Preheat your grill to medium-high heat.
2. **Prepare the Vegetables:**
   - Wash the zucchini and cherry tomatoes thoroughly.
   - Cut the zucchinis into 1-inch rounds.
3. **Skewer the Vegetables:**
   - Alternate threading zucchini rounds and cherry tomatoes onto skewers.
4. **Season and Oil:**
   - In a small bowl, mix canola oil, salt, and pepper.
   - Brush the oil mixture lightly over the skewered vegetables.
5. **Grill the Skewers:**
   - Place the skewers on the preheated grill.
   - Grill for about 5 minutes on each side or until the vegetables are tender and slightly charred.
6. **Garnish and Serve:**
   - Remove the skewers from the grill and garnish with fresh basil leaves before serving.

Nutritional Facts: Calories: 110 | Protein: 3g | Carbohydrates: 11g | Fiber: 3g | Sugars: 8g | Fat: 7g | Saturated Fat: 0.6g | Cholesterol: 0mg | Sodium: 15mg | Potassium: 550mg

Chilled Shrimp Skewers with Lemon and Herb Drizzle

Preparation time: 20 minutes; Cooking time: 5 minutes; Serving size: 2 servings

Ingredients:

For the Shrimp Skewers:

- 12 large shrimp, peeled and deveined
- 1 teaspoon grapeseed oil
- Salt and pepper to taste

For the Lemon and Herb Drizzle:

- Juice of 1 lemon
- 1 teaspoon chopped fresh parsley
- 1 teaspoon chopped fresh chives
- Salt and pepper to taste
- 1 teaspoon grapeseed oil

Instructions:

1. **Prepare the Shrimp:**
   - Preheat your grill or grill pan to medium-high heat.
   - In a bowl, toss the shrimp with grapeseed oil, salt, and pepper.
   - Thread the shrimp onto skewers.
2. **Grill the Shrimp:**
   - Place the shrimp skewers on the grill and cook for about 2-3 minutes, or until they are pink and opaque.
   - Once cooked, remove from the grill and let them cool.
3. **Prepare Lemon and Herb Drizzle:**
   - In a small bowl, combine lemon juice, chopped parsley, chopped chives, salt, and pepper. Slowly whisk in the grapeseed oil until emulsified.
4. **Assemble and Serve:**
   - Arrange the chilled shrimp skewers on a platter.
   - Drizzle the lemon and herb mixture over the shrimp.
   - Serve immediately, optionally garnished with additional herbs.

Nutritional Facts: Calories: 150 | Protein: 20g | Carbohydrates: 2g | Fiber: 0g | Sugars: 1g | Fat: 7g | Saturated Fat: 1g | Cholesterol: 180mg | Sodium: 200mg | Potassium: 90mg

Apple and Walnut Stuffed Endive Leaves

Preparation time: 20 minutes; Cooking time: 0 minutes; Serving size: 2 servings

Ingredients:

- 1 head Belgian endive, leaves separated and washed
- 1 medium apple, finely diced
- 1/4 cup chopped walnuts
- 1/2 cup low-fat Greek yogurt
- 1 teaspoon lemon juice
- Salt to taste
- Fresh parsley leaves for garnish (optional)

Instructions:

1. **Prepare the Filling:**
   - In a bowl, combine finely diced apple and chopped walnuts.
   - Add lemon juice and toss to combine.
2. **Prepare the Yogurt Mixture:**
   - In another bowl, mix low-fat Greek yogurt and a pinch of salt.
   - Stir until well blended.
3. **Assemble the Endive Leaves:**
   - Carefully spoon the apple and walnut mixture onto each endive leaf, aiming to fill the natural "cup" in the leaf.
   - Drizzle or dollop a small amount of the yogurt mixture on top of the mixture in each leaf.
4. **Garnish and Serve:**
   - Optionally, garnish with fresh parsley leaves.
   - Serve immediately, as a delightful appetizer or snack.

Nutritional Facts: Calories: 150 | Protein: 6g | Carbohydrates: 18g | Fiber: 4g | Sugars: 12g | Fat: 6g | Saturated Fat: 1g | Cholesterol: 3mg | Sodium: 60mg | Potassium: 250mg

Steamed Dumplings with Chicken and Cabbage

Preparation time: 30 minutes; Cooking time: 15 minutes; Serving size: 2 servings

Ingredients:

- 8 whole-grain dumpling wrappers
- 1 cup ground chicken breast
- 1 cup shredded Napa cabbage
- 1 tablespoon minced ginger
- 1 tablespoon minced garlic
- 1 teaspoon low-sodium soy sauce
- 1 teaspoon canola oil
- Salt to taste
- Water for steaming

Instructions:

1. **Prepare the Filling**:
   - In a mixing bowl, combine ground chicken, shredded Napa cabbage, minced ginger, and minced garlic.
   - Add low-sodium soy sauce and mix well.
2. **Wrap the Dumplings**:
   - Lay a dumpling wrapper on a clean surface.
   - Place a tablespoon of the chicken and cabbage mixture in the center of the wrapper.
   - Fold and seal the edges to create a dumpling shape.
   - Repeat with the remaining wrappers and filling.
3. **Steam the Dumplings**:
   - Add water to a steamer and bring it to a boil.
   - Brush the steamer basket with canola oil to prevent sticking.
   - Place the dumplings in the steamer basket, making sure they are not touching.
   - Cover and steam for about 15 minutes, or until the chicken is fully cooked.
4. **Serve**:
   - Carefully remove the dumplings from the steamer.
   - Serve hot, optionally with a side of low-sodium soy sauce for dipping.

Nutritional Facts: Calories: 220 | Protein: 20g | Carbohydrates: 24g | Fiber: 2g | Sugars: 1g | Fat: 4g | Saturated Fat: 0.5g | Cholesterol: 45mg | Sodium: 300mg | Potassium: 300mg

Summer Garden Gazpacho

Preparation time: 20 minutes; Cooking time: 0 minutes (chilling time: 2 hours); Serving size: 2 servings

Ingredients:

- 2 large ripe tomatoes, diced
- 1 cucumber, peeled and diced
- 1 red bell pepper, diced
- 1/2 red onion, diced
- 2 cups low-sodium vegetable broth
- Juice of 1 lemon
- 1 clove garlic, minced
- Salt to taste
- Fresh parsley or chives for garnish (optional)
- A dash of black pepper (optional, for those who can tolerate)

Instructions:

1. **Prepare Vegetables**:
   - Dice the tomatoes, cucumber, red bell pepper, and red onion.
   - Mince the garlic.
2. **Combine Ingredients**:
   - In a blender, combine the diced tomatoes, cucumber, red bell pepper, red onion, garlic, lemon juice, and low-sodium vegetable broth.
3. **Blend**:
   - Pulse a few times if you like your gazpacho chunky, or blend until smooth if you prefer it that way.
4. **Season**:
   - Add salt to taste, and a dash of black pepper if you can tolerate it.
5. **Chill**:
   - Pour the mixture into a bowl and refrigerate for at least 2 hours to allow the flavors to meld together.
6. **Garnish and Serve**:
   - Once chilled, give the gazpacho a good stir.
   - Garnish with fresh parsley or chives before serving if desired.

Nutritional Facts: Calories: 90 | Protein: 2g | Carbohydrates: 20g | Fiber: 4g | Sugars: 12g | Fat: 1g | Saturated Fat: 0g | Cholesterol: 0mg | Sodium: 200mg | Potassium: 400mg

Chapter 6: A 28-Day Meal Plan for a Gallbladder-Free Lifestyle

6.1 Explanation of how to follow the 28-day plan

Adjusting to life without a gallbladder can feel overwhelming, but rest assured: you're not alone. One of the best ways to manage your new dietary needs and regain a sense of normalcy is through a structured meal plan. That's where this chapter comes in handy. The 28-day meal plan outlined in the following pages aims to provide you with a comprehensive guide to navigate the complexities of your post-surgery nutritional requirements.

Why a 28-Day Meal Plan?

The 28-day time frame serves multiple purposes. First, it allows enough time for you to adapt to new dietary guidelines, helping you to establish healthier eating habits. Second, this duration often coincides with post-operative medical follow-ups, allowing you and your healthcare team to assess how well you're managing your diet and make any necessary adjustments. Finally, a 28-day plan is long enough to introduce variety without becoming overwhelming, helping you understand which foods agree with you and which ones to avoid.

Who is this Meal Plan For?

This meal plan is intended for individuals who have recently undergone gallbladder removal surgery or cholecystectomy and for those who have been living gallbladder-free for some time but still experience digestive issues. It follows the guidelines set forth in Chapter 2.2, "Post-Surgical Diet for the Gallbladder," to ensure that the recipes are tailored to your specific needs.

How to Use This Meal Plan

Each week, you'll find a detailed breakdown of meals for each day, which includes breakfast, lunch, snacks, and dinner. Feel free to swap meals from different days if you prefer, but try to stick to the plan as closely as possible for best results.

Notes on Portion Sizes and Substitutions

While we've done our best to approximate portion sizes to meet the general nutritional needs of most adults, individual requirements may vary. If you have special dietary needs, medical conditions, or nutritional goals, please consult your healthcare provider for tailored advice. We've also provided substitution options for certain ingredients to account for allergies or personal preferences.

6.2 Detailed Weekly Menus

Week 1: Transition & Getting Acquainted

After undergoing gallbladder surgery, the first week is all about transitioning and getting acquainted with a new way of eating. It is essential to start with a diet that is gentle on the digestive system while providing all the necessary nutrients to support the body's healing process. This week's meal plan includes a selection of recipes that are low in fat, easy to digest, and packed with vitamins and minerals.

Day 1 to Day 7 Meal Plans

Day 1:

Breakfast:	Blueberry Oatmeal Smoothie with Chia Seeds
Lunch:	Kale and Quinoa Salad with Lemon-Ginger Yogurt Sauce
Snack:	Smooth Chickpea and Beetroot Hummus
Dinner:	Grilled Turkey and Pineapple Skewers

Day 2:

Breakfast:	Quinoa Breakfast Bowl with Fresh Berries
Lunch:	Shredded Carrot and Beetroot Salad
Snack:	Apple, Celery, and Walnut Salad
Dinner:	Seared Chicken with Sautéed Spinach

Day 3:

Breakfast:	Spinach and Mushroom Egg White Scramble
Lunch:	Asian-Inspired Edamame and Brown Rice Salad
Snack:	Roasted Chickpeas with Sea Salt
Dinner:	Steamed Sole with Lemon and Dill

Day 4:

Breakfast:	Almond Milk Chia Pudding with Fresh Fruit
Lunch:	Cold Lentil Salad with Steamed Vegetables
Snack:	Homemade Rice Crackers with Herbs
Dinner:	Baked Tilapia and Veggie Foil Packs

Day 5:

Breakfast:	Egg-Free Banana Pancakes
Lunch:	Roasted Sweet Potato and Black Bean Salad
Snack:	Zucchini and Carrot Fritters (Oil-Free)
Dinner:	Herb-Roasted Chicken Breasts with Steamed Asparagus

Day 6:

Breakfast:	Steel-Cut Oats with Sliced Apple and a Drizzle of Honey
Lunch:	Strawberry and Spinach Salad with Balsamic Reduction
Snack:	Oatmeal and Raisin Cookies (No Sugar Added)
Dinner:	Lean Turkey Meatballs with Zucchini Spaghetti

Day 7:

Breakfast:	Baked Sweet Potato and Black Bean Hash
Lunch:	Tofu and Vegetable Poke Bowl
Snack:	Peach and Raspberry Gelatin Cups
Dinner:	Rosemary and Garlic Cod with Steamed Green Beans

This week is all about gentle transition, and by the end of the week, you'll be well-acquainted with the gallbladder-free lifestyle. Remember to drink plenty of water throughout the day and adjust portion sizes to suit your individual needs. If you have any food intolerances or allergies, be sure to modify the recipes accordingly. Happy eating!

Week 2: Introducing Variety

Now that you are acquainted with the gallbladder-free lifestyle, week two is all about introducing a variety of foods to your diet. It is important to maintain a balanced diet with a wide range of nutrients to support your body's healing process. This week's meal plan includes a diverse selection of recipes that are not only nutritious but also delicious and satisfying.

Day 8 to Day 14 Meal Plans

Day 8:
Breakfast:	Overnight Soaked Millet with Fresh Mango
Lunch:	Garlic-Free Chickpea and Spinach Curry
Snack:	Almond Milk Rice Pudding with Vanilla Bean
Dinner:	Poached Rainbow Trout with Fresh Herbs

Day 9:
Breakfast:	Vegetable Omelette with Dairy-Free Cheese
Lunch:	Asian-Inspired Edamame and Brown Rice Salad
Snack:	Zesty Orange and Pineapple Ice Pops
Dinner:	Skinless Chicken Stir-Fry with Polenta

Day 10:
Breakfast:	Steel-Cut Oats with Sliced Apple and a Drizzle of Honey
Lunch:	Tofu and Vegetable Poke Bowl
Snack:	Garlic-Free Quinoa and Spinach Balls
Dinner:	Herb-Crusted Haddock with Steamed Asparagus

Day 11:
Breakfast:	Spinach and Mushroom Egg White Scramble
Lunch:	Lentil and Spinach Stew
Snack:	Baked Sweet Potato Fries with Paprika
Dinner:	Black Bean Tacos with Cabbage Slaw

Day 12:
Breakfast:	Blueberry Oatmeal Smoothie with Chia Seeds
Lunch:	Strawberry and Spinach Salad with Balsamic Reduction
Snack:	Homemade Banana and Blueberry Sorbet
Dinner:	Halibut Skewers with Zucchini and Bell Peppers

Day 13:
Breakfast:	Egg-Free Banana Pancakes
Lunch:	Tomato Basil Soup with Brown Rice
Snack:	Peach and Raspberry Gelatin Cups
Dinner:	Lean Turkey Loaf with Roasted Sweet Potatoes

Day 14:
Breakfast:	Quinoa Breakfast Bowl with Fresh Berries
Lunch:	Cold Lentil Salad with Steamed Vegetables
Snack:	Vegan Chocolate Avocado Mousse
Dinner:	Tempeh and Brown Rice Stir-fry with Steamed Veggies

In this second week, you are encouraged to enjoy a variety of foods, while still keeping an eye on portion sizes and making modifications for any food intolerances or allergies. Continue to drink plenty of water and stay active to support your body's healing process. This is a great time to notice how your body is responding to different foods and make any necessary adjustments to your diet. Stay committed to your health and well-being!

Week 3: Building Balanced Habits

Congratulations on completing two weeks of the gallbladder-free lifestyle meal plan! By now, you should have become more comfortable with the variety of foods and meals that support your health. Week 3 is about building on those habits, maintaining the variety in your diet, and finding the balance that works best for you. Remember, the key to a successful diet is consistency and balance.

Day 15 to Day 21 Meal Plans

Day 15:
Breakfast:	Baked Sweet Potato and Black Bean Hash
Lunch:	Cream-Free Mushroom and Asparagus Risotto
Snack:	Peach and Almond Milk Smoothie
Dinner:	Seared Chicken with Sautéed Spinach

Day 16:
Breakfast:	Almond Milk Chia Pudding with Fresh Fruit
Lunch:	Tuna Steak Salad with Mixed Greens
Snack:	Smooth Chickpea and Beetroot Hummus
Dinner:	Balsamic Glazed Chicken and Quinoa Salad

Day 17:
Breakfast:	Overnight Soaked Millet with Fresh Mango
Lunch:	Roasted Sweet Potato and Black Bean Salad
Snack:	Baked Pears with a Drizzle of Maple Syrup
Dinner:	Steamed Sole with Lemon and Dill

Day 18:
Breakfast:	Vegetable Omelette with Dairy-Free Cheese
Lunch:	Cauliflower Soup with Shrimps
Snack:	Homemade Rice Crackers with Herbs
Dinner:	Spiced but Not Spicy Catfish with Quinoa

Day 19:
Breakfast:	Quinoa Breakfast Bowl with Fresh Berries
Lunch:	Apple, Celery, and Walnut Salad
Snack:	Vegan Chocolate Avocado Mousse
Dinner:	Lean Turkey Meatballs with Zucchini Spaghetti

Day 20:
Breakfast:	Steel-Cut Oats with Sliced Apple and a Drizzle of Honey
Lunch:	Kale and Quinoa Salad with Lemon-Ginger Yogurt Sauce
Snack:	Zesty Orange and Pineapple Ice Pops
Dinner:	Herb-Roasted Chicken Breasts with Steamed Asparagus

Day 21:
Breakfast:	Spinach and Mushroom Egg White Scramble
Lunch:	Asian-Style Tofu and Bok Choy Soup
Snack:	Oatmeal and Raisin Cookies (No Sugar Added)
Dinner:	Rosemary and Garlic Cod with Steamed Green Beans

Maintaining a balanced diet is essential for overall health, especially when adjusting to a gallbladder-free lifestyle. In this week, you have continued to introduce a variety of nutrients while keeping portion sizes and food intolerances in mind. You are encouraged to maintain hydration, stay active, and adjust portions and food choices based on how your body responds. Remember, this meal plan is a guideline, and it's important to listen to your body and adjust as necessary. Keep up the great work and stay committed to your health and well-being!

Week 4: Mastering the Gallbladder-Free Lifestyle

Welcome to the final week of your 28-day meal plan for a gallbladder-free lifestyle. By now, you have transitioned into this new lifestyle, introduced a variety of foods, and built balanced habits. This week is all about mastering this lifestyle, listening to your body, and making adjustments as needed. Remember, the goal is to create a sustainable, healthy eating pattern that you can maintain long-term.

Day 22 to Day 28 Meal Plans

Day 22:
Breakfast:	Quinoa Breakfast Bowl with Fresh Berries
Lunch:	Cold Lentil Salad with Steamed Vegetables
Snack:	Peachy Keen: Peach and Almond Milk Smoothie
Dinner:	Garlic-Free Chickpea and Spinach Curry

Day 23:
Breakfast:	Blueberry Oatmeal Smoothie with Chia Seeds
Lunch:	Tofu and Vegetable Poke Bowl
Snack:	Steamed Asparagus Spears with Lemon Zest
Dinner:	Halibut Skewers with Zucchini and Bell Peppers

Day 24:
Breakfast:	Vegetable Omelette with Dairy-Free Cheese
Lunch:	Vegetable Barley Soup
Snack:	Gluten-Free Apple Crumble with Oat Topping
Dinner:	Chicken Fajita Stuffed Bell Peppers

Day 25:
Breakfast:	Egg-Free Banana Pancakes
Lunch:	Strawberry and Spinach Salad with Balsamic Reduction
Snack:	Mango Tango: Mango and Coconut Water Smoothie
Dinner:	Poached Rainbow Trout with Fresh Herbs

Day 26:
Breakfast:	Steel-Cut Oats with Sliced Apple and a Drizzle of Honey
Lunch:	Asian-Inspired Edamame and Brown Rice Salad
Snack:	Almond Milk Rice Pudding with Vanilla Bean
Dinner:	Skinless Chicken Stir-Fry with Polenta

Day 27:
Breakfast:	Baked Sweet Potato and Black Bean Hash
Lunch:	Mushroom and Leek Clear Soup
Snack:	Zucchini and Carrot Fritters (Oil-Free)
Dinner:	Herb-Crusted Haddock with Steamed Asparagus

Day 28:
Breakfast:	Overnight Soaked Millet with Fresh Mango
Lunch:	Apple, Celery, and Walnut Salad
Snack:	Zesty Orange and Pineapple Ice Pops
Dinner:	Grilled Turkey and Pineapple Skewers

In this final week, you have continued to focus on balance, variety, and portion control while incorporating all the learned strategies into your daily routine. By now, you should feel more comfortable and confident in making food choices that support your gallbladder-free lifestyle. Remember, the journey doesn't end here. It's important to continue listening to your body, making adjustments as needed, and seeking guidance from healthcare professionals if necessary. Congratulations on completing the 28-day meal plan and taking control of your health and well-being!

Chapter 7: A Journey Beyond Surgery

Living without a gallbladder presents new challenges but also offers opportunities for enhanced well-being. While a gallbladder-free life often requires dietary changes and lifestyle adaptations, it is perfectly possible to live a full and happy life. This closing chapter addresses some of the emotional and psychological aspects of life post-gallbladder surgery, as well as guidance for long-term wellness.

Recognizing and Managing Post-Surgery Anxiety and Stress

It's entirely natural to experience a degree of anxiety and stress following surgery. Your body has gone through a significant change, and it's understandable to be concerned about the "new normal." Many people worry about the kind of foods they can eat, possible weight changes, and overall health. The key is not to let this anxiety govern your life.

When it comes to managing post-surgery anxiety, one thing that can make a world of difference is **professional help**. You know your own mental state best, and if you feel that the emotional toll is becoming too much to bear alone, seeking guidance from a mental health professional who has experience in dealing with surgical stress can offer invaluable insights and coping strategies.

Now, let's talk about **mindfulness techniques**. These are not just buzzwords but effective tools that you can incorporate into your daily routine. Simple practices like breathing exercises can significantly reduce stress levels. Meditation, for even just a few minutes each day, can provide a sense of calm and help focus your thoughts away from anxious feelings.

Physical activity can be another great stress-reliever, but this comes with a big asterisk: **Always consult your doctor** before diving into any exercise routine after surgery. Gentle, doctor-approved exercise, such as walking, can lift your mood and help counteract stress, providing both physical and emotional benefits.

Another incredible resource is the community around you. **Support groups**, both online and in-person, offer a safe space to share your experiences, concerns, and victories. Sometimes, the mere act of verbalizing what you're going through can offer a sense of relief, not to mention the comfort that comes from knowing you're not alone.

Remember, it's okay to ask for help and it's okay to prioritize your mental health. Your post-surgery journey is not just about physical healing, but emotional and mental well-being, too.

How to Help Loved Ones in Their Post-Surgery Journey

When someone you care about goes through surgery, especially something as significant as gallbladder removal, your first instinct is often to ask, **"How can I help?"** Well, the good news is, there are many ways to be supportive, and the first thing to remember is that **your presence itself is powerful**. Sometimes, just being there, holding a hand, or offering a listening ear can make all the difference.

Let's get real about **communication**, shall we? It's crucial to keep the lines open and encourage your loved one to express how they're feeling physically and emotionally. But this doesn't mean bombarding them with questions. Instead, let them know you're there to listen whenever they're ready to talk. Empathy goes a long way.

The concept of **"help" can be subjective**. What you think is helpful may not be what your loved one needs or wants. So, don't hesitate to ask them directly how you can be of assistance. Whether it's running errands, cooking meals, or just giving them some alone time, your willingness to adapt to their needs will be highly appreciated.

Taking on the role of an **information ally** can be incredibly helpful. This means you could assist in researching post-surgery care, accompanying them to follow-up appointments, or helping keep track of medications and symptoms. Keep in mind that medical jargon can be overwhelming, so your role might also include breaking down information into more digestible pieces.

Now, what about the emotional roller coaster that comes post-surgery? Be prepared for mood swings and emotional days; they're par for the course. Emotional support is often as important as physical care. So, consider activities that can uplift their spirit. Maybe it's watching a favorite movie together, enjoying some light humor, or simply sharing moments of silence.

Lastly, let's talk about **setting boundaries**. You want to help, but you also have your own life and responsibilities. It's okay to set limits and take time for yourself too. You'll be of no help to anyone if you're burned out. So, maintain a balance and don't be shy about seeking additional help if needed.

Helping a loved one through their post-surgery journey is an act of love, but it's also a responsibility that you should approach with both care and thoughtfulness. Remember, every little bit counts, and sometimes the smallest gestures can have the most significant impact.

Recognizing Signs of Potential Issues and When to Seek Medical Advice

Even with a successful surgery and a well-managed lifestyle, it's essential to remain vigilant for any signs of complications or other health issues. The body can sometimes present subtle cues that something isn't right, and early detection is crucial for effective treatment. Here's what to keep an eye on:

Physical Symptoms:

- **Unexplained Pain**: Any persistent or severe pain in the abdominal area should not be ignored.
- **Digestive Issues**: Frequent nausea, vomiting, or severe indigestion can be a warning sign.
- **Changes in Bowel Movements**: Consistently abnormal stools, especially if bloody or black, warrant a consultation with a healthcare provider.
- **Jaundice**: Yellowing of the skin or eyes is a significant concern and requires immediate medical attention.

Behavioral Changes:

- **Loss of Appetite**: A sudden and unexplained loss of appetite might be indicative of a digestive issue.
- **Excessive Fatigue**: While some tiredness is normal, extreme fatigue is not and could signal an underlying issue.
- **Unexplained Weight Loss**: If you're shedding pounds without trying, this is cause for concern.

Emotional Signs:

- **Increased Anxiety or Stress**: While some stress is expected post-surgery, increasing or persistent stress and anxiety can sometimes point to a deeper issue.
- **Depression**: Feelings of extreme sadness, disinterest in activities, or significant changes in sleep patterns should be addressed with a healthcare provider.

When to Seek Medical Advice:

- **Consistent Symptoms**: If you experience any of these symptoms consistently over a period, it's advisable to seek medical attention.
- **Escalating Severity**: Any symptom that starts mild but becomes severe should be addressed immediately.
- **Multiple Symptoms**: The occurrence of multiple symptoms simultaneously is a strong indicator that medical advice is needed.

Remember, you know your body best. **Trust your instincts**. If something feels off, it's always better to consult with your healthcare provider sooner rather than later. It's not just about tackling issues as they arise but taking a proactive approach to maintain your health.

Maintaining a Balanced Lifestyle for Years to Come

Let's get one thing straight: Surgery may be behind you, but this is just the beginning of a new chapter. It's the perfect time to take stock and think about the kind of lifestyle that will best serve you going forward. You might be tempted to ease back into old habits, but I strongly urge you to **embrace change as your ally**.

One of the most essential shifts you can make is towards a **consistent and balanced diet**. I get it, indulgences are hard to resist. But small, consistent choices add up. Consider incorporating whole, natural foods, like fruits, vegetables, and lean proteins into your meals. And don't forget to hydrate; yes, good old water is your best friend here.

Now let's talk about **exercise**. Don't let the word scare you; it doesn't have to mean grueling hours at the gym. Even a simple walk around the block, some stretching, or light yoga can make a big difference. The key is to be consistent. Consistency not only improves your physical health but also does wonders for your mental state.

Annual medical check-ups, including liver function tests and full blood count, can help monitor your health in the long run. It's not just about absence of illness but ensuring you're thriving in your gallbladder-free life.

All these elements might seem overwhelming at first, but the key is to **start small and build up**. Give yourself grace as you navigate this new way of living, but also hold yourself accountable. Balancing health with life's pleasures is indeed an art form, but with some practice and a lot of self-love, you'll get there. So here's to you, your health, and the many fulfilling years you have ahead!

Conclusion

Congratulations on making it to the end of this journey! By seeking out this book, you have shown a remarkable commitment to your health and well-being after gallbladder surgery. Whether you are seeking guidance after your recent surgery, curious and eager to understand the complexities of life after gallbladder removal, or supportive and willing to provide the best possible care for a loved one, you have taken an important step toward a healthier gallbladder-free lifestyle.

This book was designed as a comprehensive tool to navigate the complexities of life after gallbladder surgery. It has provided you with essential knowledge about the gallbladder, the physiological changes that occur after surgery, and how to manage potential complications. You have also been equipped with a plethora of nutritional recommendations and delicious recipes that cater to a gallbladder-free lifestyle. The 28-day meal plan was created to ease the transition into this new way of life and help build balanced eating habits. Moreover, the book has also touched upon the emotional and psychological aspects of the post-surgery journey, offering advice on managing anxiety and stress, supporting loved ones, and maintaining a balanced lifestyle in the long run.

Remember, this book is not just a one-time read, but a resource you can return to time and time again as you continue on your journey towards optimal health. Thank you for allowing this book to be a part of your path to wellness. Here's to a healthier, happier, gallbladder-free life!

References

Donato F. Altomare, Maria T. Rotelli , Nicola Palasciano (2019). Diet After Cholecystectomy. Curr. Med. Chem. 2019;26(19):3662-3665.

Yongju Shin, Dongho Choi, Kyeong Geun Lee, Ho Soon Choi, Yongsoon Park (2018). Association between dietary intake and postlaparoscopic cholecystectomic symptoms in patients with gallbladder disease. Korean J Intern Med. 2018 Jul;33(4):829-836.

Poyoung Shim, Dongho Choi, Yongsoon Park (2017). Association of Blood Fatty Acid Composition and Dietary Pattern with the Risk of Non-Alcoholic Fatty Liver Disease in Patients Who Underwent Cholecystectomy. Ann Nutr Metab. 2017;70(4):303-311.

P. K. Nguyen, S. Lin, P. Heidenreich (2016). A systematic comparison of sugar content in low-fat vs regular versions of food. Nutr Diabetes. 2016 Jan; 6(1): e193.

Nefise Çalişkan, Hülya Bulut, Ali Konan (2016). The Effect of Warm Water Intake on Bowel Movements in the Early Postoperative Stage of Patients Having Undergone Laparoscopic Cholecystectomy: A Randomized Controlled Trial. Gastroenterol Nurs. 2016 Sep-Oct;39(5):340-7.

Chantal Housset, Yues Chrétien, Dominique Debray, Nicolas Chignard (2016). Functions of the Gallbladder. Compr Physiol. 2016 Jun 13;6(3):1549-77.

Przemysław Jacek Galbfach, Marta Bozenna Kołacińska, Paweł Arkadiusz Flont, Michał Igor Spychalski, Piotr Gustaw Narbutt, Michal Lukasz Mik, Łukasz Adam Dziki, Adam Janusz Dziki (2008). Gastric complaints or postcholecystectomy syndrome?. Pol Merkur Lekarski. 2008 Sep;25(147):221-5.

Printed in Great Britain
by Amazon